Watchman's Mini Guide to

The Antichrist

By Richard H. Perry

"I am Yahweh, who carries out the words of his servants and fulfills the predictions of his messengers"

(Isaiah 44:24, 26)

Watchman's Mini Guide to

The Antichrist

Copyright © 2013, Richard H. Perry

All Rights Reserved. No part of this publication may be reproduced, stored in a retrieval system or transmitted in any form or by any means-electronic, mechanical, photocopy, recording or any other-except for brief quotations in printed reviews, without prior permission by the author.

All Scripture quotations are from the Holy Bible, New International Version, Copyright © 1973, 1978, 1984 International Bible Society. Used with permission of Zondervan Publishing House. All rights Reserved. **Bold lettering** has been added for emphasis and the name **Yahweh** has been inserted in the place of the title "**the LORD**" which better reflects the Hebrew name of Almighty God. The Hebrew title "Messiah" and the Greek title "Christ" will be used interchangeably.

Website:	www.lastdaysmystery.info
Email:	lastdaysmystery@yahoo.com
Youtube:	richardperry2
Twitter:	richardperry2

Table of Contents:

Author		4
Introduction		6
Chapter 1	Titles of the Antichrist	8
Chapter 2	First the Kingdom	16
Chapter 3	Kingdom with Ten Kings	26
Chapter 4	When Rebels become Terrorists	32
Chapter 5	First Antichrist Wars	41
Chapter 6	Antichrist's Last 7 Years	53
Chapter 7	Antichrist's Last 3.5 Years	77
Chapter 8	Seal Wars before Antichrist	87
Chapter 9	Seal Wars with Antichrist	120
Chapter 10	More about Antichrist	150
Books by Richard H. Perry		178

Richard H. Perry

I have studied the Bible for over thirty-three years. In the past twelve years my focus has been on the Time of the End, the Second Coming of the Messiah and biblical repentance.

Served as church elder, foreign missionary with Habitat for Humanity International, Vice-President of a local Full Gospel Businessmen's Fellowship International and taught biblical studies on the Time of the End to groups inside and outside the organized church.

Studied at Elim Bible Institute and holds Bachelor of Science degree from Rochester Institute of Technology.

Since 2001, Yahweh, the God of the Bible, has led me to write several books about the Last Days, the Time of the End and the Second Coming of Christ. During the past twelve years Yahweh has taught me many things from Scripture. Perhaps the most important lesson has been to set aside the teachings and traditions of man in favor of Yahweh and His Word.

In 2003 Yahweh made it clear to me that I was to be a Watchman for His people. The books I have written are primarily about the wars that will occur during the Time of the End and the Repentance which Yahweh requires.

In 2002 I launched the website LastDaysMystery.info. I also produce videos for YouTube and post articles and news releases on Facebook and Twitter. I've appeared on History Channel about the Rapture and from time to time I conduct prophecy conferences on the Time of the End and the Second Coming of the Messiah, called Jesus Christ.

In 2012, I released the "Watchman's Guide" series of books which now includes the following topics:

- The Time of the End
- The Rapture
- Revelation
- Daniel's Prophecies +
- End Time Repentance
- End Time U.S.A.
- The Antichrist

Introduction

"Watchman's Guide to the Antichrist" is the latest in a series concerning biblical prophecy about the Time of the End and the Second Coming of the Messiah. In it we will examine what I understand from Yahweh, the God of the Bible, concerning the Antichrist and the Time of the End.

I am writing this book concerning what Scripture says about the Antichrist because of the great amount of misinformation which has been spread concerning this critically important End Time figure. In spite of the fact that the Antichrist is the most prophetically described End Time character; he is relatively unknown to Christians today. This is because Christian's generally don't read Scripture and rely heavily on the teachings of man and organized religion to guide their beliefs. They do this even though the Bible warns them against trusting in man.

The teachings I have received from Yahweh are different from what has been preached and taught in organized religion. However, Yahweh has shown me the harmony of biblical prophecy concerning the Antichrist and the Time of the End and I will pass that along so you can see what I see in Scripture.

As we examine Scripture, I will point out the following concerning what I have been taught about the Antichrist:

Concerning the Antichrist

- His titles
- How he arises to world power.
- From where he arises to power.
- When he arises to power.
- When he will be revealed.
- What he will do.
- What he looks like.
- How he comes to his end.

I will also be addressing how I have been taught to read and understand Scripture and discuss how to know from the Bible that the Time of the End has come and when the Antichrist will appear on the scene.

What I have been taught can be confirmed by a careful examination of Scripture, as led by the Holy Spirit. However, very soon Iran will take peace from the earth as described in Revelation 6:3-4. This will likely happen when Iran ambushes U.S. Navy Carrier Strike Groups in the Persian Gulf region, off the Iranian coast.

Soon after this war begins and the resulting economic crisis ensues, God's people will wake up and be able to see these prophesied events in Scripture and confirm for themselves that what I am saying is true.

Now, let's see what is required to read and understand the Word of God!

Chapter 1

Titles of the Antichrist

Bible prophecy provides a considerable amount of information concerning the man we call "the Antichrist." The Antichrist is also the predominant Time of the End figure described in biblical prophecy until the return of the Messiah, called Christ. However, "Antichrist" is not the only title which the prophets used when describing this Time of the End leader. His titles are important and can be helpful to our understanding about this man. We should consider these titles carefully.

Let's start with his most popular title first.

Antichrist

The title "Antichrist" has become very popular in identifying the Time of the End world leader. This title was only used in Scripture by the apostle John in his first two epistles. Even though John wrote the book of Revelation he did not use the title Antichrist again. Let's learn what we can from John's description of the Antichrist.

> "Dear children, this is the last hour; and as you have heard that **the antichrist is coming** ..." (1 John 2:18)

> "Who is the liar? It is the man who denies that Jesus is the Christ [the Messiah]. Such a man is **the antichrist--he denies the Father and the Son.**" (1 John 2:22)

From John's description we learn that the "Antichrist" is a man, he is a liar, he will deny that Yeshua (Jesus) is the Messiah and he will deny that Yahweh is the Father. By denying Yahweh and Yeshua, the Antichrist will in effect deny the God of the Bible.

John also indicated that other individuals can have the spirit of antichrist. But there will only be one Time of the End world leader who is the "Antichrist".

The "Antichrist" and the "Beast" king of the fourth Middle-eastern kingdom, are the same person. Daniel was given six Time of the End prophecies and each of them dealt in some way with the final "Beast" king or his kingdom. These six prophecies are recorded in Daniel chapters; 2, 7, 8, 9, 11 and 12.

Let's take a look at a passage below which connects the "Antichrist" as described by John with the beast king of Daniel.

> "The king will do as he pleases. He will exalt and magnify himself above every god and will say unheard-of things against the God of gods. He will be successful until the time of wrath is completed, for what has been determined must take place. He will show no regard for the gods of his fathers or for the one desired by women, nor will he regard any god, but will exalt himself above them all." (Daniel 11:36-37)

In this passage, Yahweh is God and Yeshua is the one desired by women. Therefore, as we read in 1 John 2:22, "the man who denies ... the Father and the Son" is the "Antichrist." Here in Daniel's prophecy we see that the king, denies them both and exalts himself above all gods. Therefore, based on Scripture, this final world ruler of Daniel's prophecies will be the coming "Antichrist."

Before we look at the other titles of the Antichrist, let's consider this title carefully.

The title Antichrist makes some people think that this man will be the false Messiah, or false Christ. This makes them think that the Antichrist will be Christ like. However, we will see as we examine Scripture about the Antichrist that he will not have Christ like characteristics. He will be a warrior king who causes great destruction of men and nations. The only biblical similarity between Christ and the Antichrist is that they both claim to be God.

When thinking about the title Antichrist, it would be best if we think of the title literally. The Antichrist will be Anti (against) Christ, not Christ like.

Antichrist also has other titles.

The Beast King

This final world ruler is also called the "Beast" king. He will rise to power from a kingdom which is also referred to as the "Beast." One Beast is the king and the other is his kingdom. Normally the distinction between the two beasts is apparent in the written description. Here is an example of the Beast, who is a king:

> "Then I continued to watch because of the boastful words the horn [king] was speaking. I kept looking until **the beast** was slain and **its body** destroyed and thrown into the blazing fire." (Daniel 7:11)

As we see in this example the king (horn) is the "Beast King" the man also known as the "Antichrist."

We also find the beast title for antichrist used in Revelation's prophecies. Blow are two example:

> "The beast was given a mouth to utter proud words and blasphemies and to exercise its authority for forty-two months." (Revelation 13:5)

> "The beast and the ten horns you saw will hate the prostitute. They will bring her to ruin and leave her naked; they will eat her flesh and burn her with fire." (Revelation 17:16)

What else has the Antichrist been called?

Ruler Who Will Come

The prophet Daniel also referred to the "Antichrist" as "the ruler who will come". In one of his Time of the End prophecies, Daniel used the title "the ruler who will come" when he was writing about the people (ancestors) of the Antichrist. In this prophecy, Daniel identified the ancestry of the future Antichrist. He said the Antichrist would be of the people who will destroy Jerusalem and the Temple, as we read here:

> "The people, of **the ruler who will come,** will destroy the city and the sanctuary." (Daniel 9:26)

In this prophecy Daniel indicated that the Antichrist will be from the people of Ancient Syria, because the ancient Syrians were the people who destroyed the city and the sanctuary in 70 A.D.

As we previously read in chapter two, this prophecy from Daniel confirms that "the ruler who will come" is the Antichrist. We can confirm that "the ruler who will come" is the Antichrist from the next verse in Daniel's prophecy. The next verse describes the Antichrist's key activities during the last seven years, as we read below:

> "He [Antichrist] will confirm a covenant with many for one 'seven.' In the middle of the 'seven' he will put an end to sacrifice and offering. And on a wing of the temple **he will set up an abomination that causes desolation**, until the end that is decreed is poured out on him." (Daniel 9:27)

There is another title for the Antichrist that we should know.

Man of Lawlessness

The apostle Paul in the New Testament used this title for the Antichrist when he was describing what would happen at the "abomination that causes desolation". Here is how Paul identified the Antichrist as the "Man of Lawlessness":

> "that day will not come until ...**the man of lawlessness** is revealed, the man doomed to destruction. He will oppose and will exalt himself over everything that is called God or is worshiped, so that **he sets himself up in God's temple, proclaiming himself to be Go**d." (2 Thessalonians 2:3-4)

This event called the "abomination that causes desolation" will take place in the Jewish Temple of Yahweh. It is the same event described in Daniel 9:27, which we just read above. This same event was also referred in Matthew 24:15 and indicated in Isaiah 10 below:

> "In that day the remnant of Israel, the survivors of Jacob, will no longer rely on him (Antichrist) who struck them down but will truly rely on Yahweh, the Holy One of Israel." (Isaiah 10:20)

At the beginning of the last seven years the Antichrist will confirm a covenant with many for Israel's security. Then in the middle of the seven the Antichrist will strike them down during the Great Tribulation.

There is another title for the Antichrist that we should know.

The Assyrian

In Isaiah and Micah, Yahweh calls the Antichrist "the Assyrian, the King of Assyria as we see below:

> "Woe to **the Assyrian**, the rod of my anger, in whose hand is the club of my wrath!" (Isaiah 10:5)

> "When the Lord has finished all his work against Mount Zion and Jerusalem, he will say, "I will punish the **king of Assyria** for the willful pride of his heart and the haughty look in his eyes." (Isaiah 10:12)

> "When **the Assyrian** invades our land and marches through our fortresses," (Micah 5:5)

There is one more title for the Antichrist that we should know.

Gog

> "This is what the Sovereign Yahweh says: I am against you, **Gog**, **chief prince** of Meshek and Tubal." (Ezekiel 38:3)

Now that we know the titles which Yahweh has used for the "Antichrist", let's examine Scripture to determine where the Antichrist comes from and how he will arise to world power.

The prophet Daniel provides a detailed account of the rise of the Beast King we know as Antichrist. In Daniel chapters 2, 7, 8, 9 and 11 the prophet describes aspects of the Antichrist's kingdom and his rise to power.

First, the kingdom must come into existence, then and only then can the Antichrist rise to power.

Chapter 2

First the Kingdom

Daniel's prophecies were written during the sixth century B.C., after the Babylonians had conquered Israel and taken Israel into captivity. Daniel received several visions and prophecies during his time in Babylon beginning when he was a youth under King Nebuchadnezzar.

Daniel's first vision and prophecy was regarding a dream King Nebuchadnezzar received from God. Yahweh also gave Daniel the vision of this dream and its interpretation to give to the king. The vision revealed that four world kingdoms would come to power before Yahweh establishes His Kingdom on earth. The first of the four kingdoms was the Babylonian Kingdom which fell to the second kingdom of Media-Persia. After Media-Persia, the third kingdom of Greece came to power under Alexander the Great. We will see as we examine Daniel's other prophecies that God actually refers to the first three kingdoms of Babylon, Media-Persia and Greece by name. Therefore, we know what parts of Daniel's prophecies have been fulfilled and what parts remain for the Time of the End.

Yahweh indicated to Daniel that after the first three kingdoms had risen and fallen, a fourth kingdom would arise. This fourth and final world kingdom, when it comes will be destroyed by God and replaced with Yahweh's eternal Kingdom on earth. This sequence holds true in each of Daniel's prophecies.

First, Daniel reveals something that Yahweh's people would do well to understand.

Only Yahweh Reveals the Future

Daniel says that only God in Heaven can reveal the mystery about what will happen in the future. No man can explain what will happen in the days to come unless God reveals it to him. The fact that God must reveal the truth to His people has been born out many times in the history of Yahweh's prophets and watchmen.

> "Unless Yahweh watches over the city, the watchmen stand guard in vain." (Psalm 127:1)

> Daniel replied, "No wise man, enchanter, magician or diviner can explain to the king the mystery he has asked about, but there is a **God in heaven who reveals mysteries.**" (Daniel 2:27-28)

Mere men without the inspiration of the Holy Spirit have a long track record of failed predictions when they speak out of their own imaginations, when they go beyond what is written. Yahweh indicates that unless the prophet stands in His council they have not been sent by Him and that their message is their own, not His.

> "I did not send these prophets, yet they have run with their message; I did not speak to them, yet they have prophesied. But **if they had stood in my council, they would have proclaimed my words to my people.**" (Jeremiah 23:21-22)

This very important warning against false prophets has been repeated by God numerous times in Scripture. It was the first warning that Christ gave His disciples concerning the Time of the End and His Second Coming.

> "Jesus answered: 'Watch out that no one deceives you. For **many will come in my name**, claiming, 'I am the Christ,' **and will deceive many.**'" (Matthew 24:4-5)

The New Testament also says that man without the Spirit cannot understand Spiritual things.

> "The man without the Spirit does not accept the things that come from the Spirit of God, for they are foolishness to him, and he cannot understand them, because they are spiritually discerned." (1 Corinthians 2:14)

Never-the-less, God reassures His people that they can read and understand His Word.

> "For we do not write you anything you cannot read or understand." (2 Corinthians 1:13)

Now, let see how Daniel describes King Nebuchadnezzar's dream.

The Dream

"You looked, O king, and there before you stood a large statue--an enormous, dazzling statue, awesome in appearance. The head of the statue was made of pure gold, its chest and arms of silver, its belly and thighs of bronze, its legs of iron, its feet partly of iron and partly of baked clay. While you were watching, a rock was cut out, but not by human hands. It struck the statue on its feet of iron and clay and smashed them. Then the iron, the clay, the bronze, the silver and the gold were broken to pieces at the same time and became like chaff on a threshing floor in the summer. The wind swept them away without leaving a trace. But the rock that struck the statue became a huge mountain and filled the whole earth." (Daniel 2:31-35)

Dream Explained

Then Daniel interpreted the dream to the king.

"**You are that head of gold**. **After you**, another kingdom will rise, inferior to yours. **Next**, a third kingdom, one of bronze, will rule over the whole earth. **Finally, there will be a fourth kingdom**, strong as iron--for iron breaks and smashes everything - and as iron breaks things to pieces, so **it will crush and break all the others**.

Just as you saw that the feet and toes were partly of baked clay and partly of iron, so this will be a divided kingdom; yet it will have some of the strength of iron in it, even as you saw iron mixed with clay. As the toes were partly iron and partly clay, so **this kingdom** will be partly strong and partly brittle. And just as you saw the iron mixed with baked clay, so **the people will be a mixture and will not remain united**, any more than iron mixes with clay. **In the time of those kings, the God of heaven will set up a kingdom** that will never be destroyed, nor will it be left to another people. **It will crush all those kingdoms and bring them to an end**, but **it will endure forever."** (Daniel 2:37-44)

First the prophecy identifies the first three kingdoms which appear from history and Daniel's prophecies to have been fulfilled by Babylon, Media-Persia and Greece. Then we are given several details about the fourth and final kingdom which will be very strong, yet its people will not remain united. This fourth kingdom will crush all other kingdoms, but will itself be crushed by God when He sets up His eternal kingdom.

Now let's take a look at the statue to learn what we can about our future. We first see three historical kingdoms of the past; Babylon, Media-Persia and Greece.

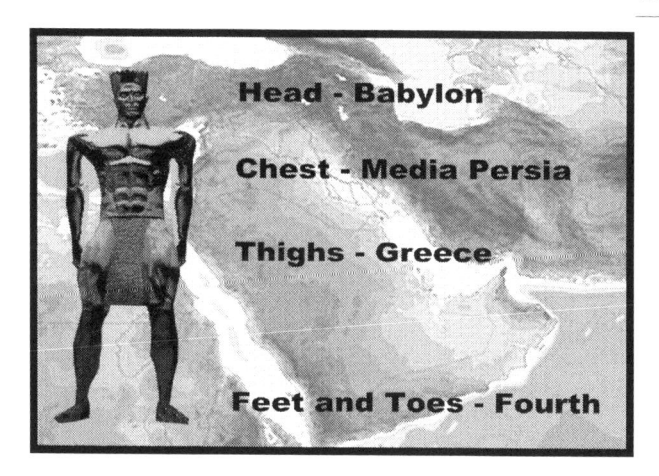

> Head - Babylon
>
> Chest - Media Persia
>
> Thighs - Greece
>
> Feet and Toes - Fourth

The statue also portrays a picture of the future because the fourth and final kingdom has not yet formed. The fourth kingdom will be the kingdom destroyed by the Messiah at His Second Coming.

Now that we have this basic picture of the statue, let's examine the geographical territories of each of the three historical kingdoms.

First Three Kingdoms

The Babylonian Empire existed from 612 to 539 BC and occupied much of the territory of the Assyrian Empire which preceded it. The Babylonian Empire encompassed the lightly shaded area depicted on the map below. The heart of the ancient empire is what we know today as Iraq.

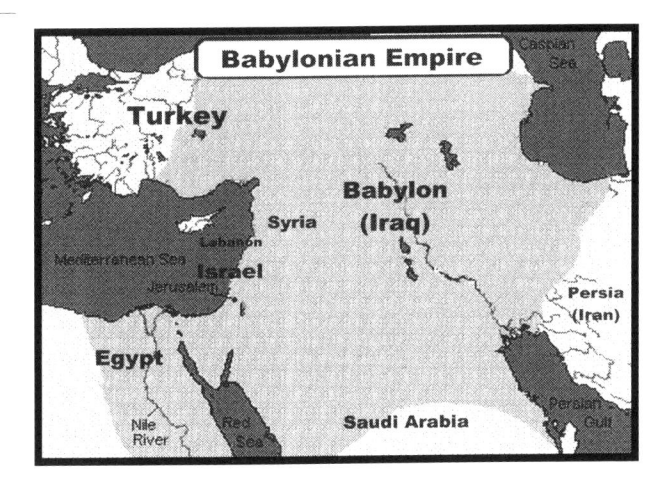

Babylon was conquered by Media-Persia which existed from 539 to 331 BC and encompassed the lightly shaded area depicted on the map below. Its capital was the city of Babylon.

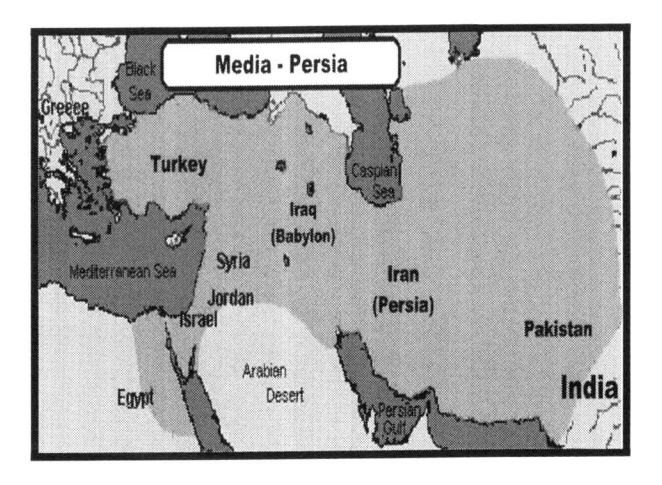

Media-Persia was conquered by Alexander the Great in 331 BC. The Greek Empire under Alexander lasted only a few years before Alexander's untimely death in 323 BC when the empire was divided between Alexander's four generals. The Greek Empire under Alexander was the largest of the historical kingdoms portrayed in the Statue and encompassed the lightly shaded area depicted on the map below. Alexander's capital remained in Babylon.

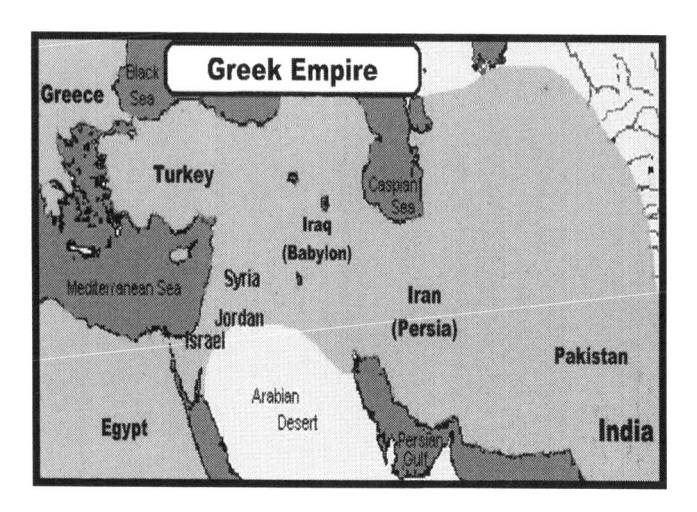

Fourth Kingdom

Getting a picture of the statue in relationship to the ancient territories covered by these first three kingdoms might today look something like this picture below.

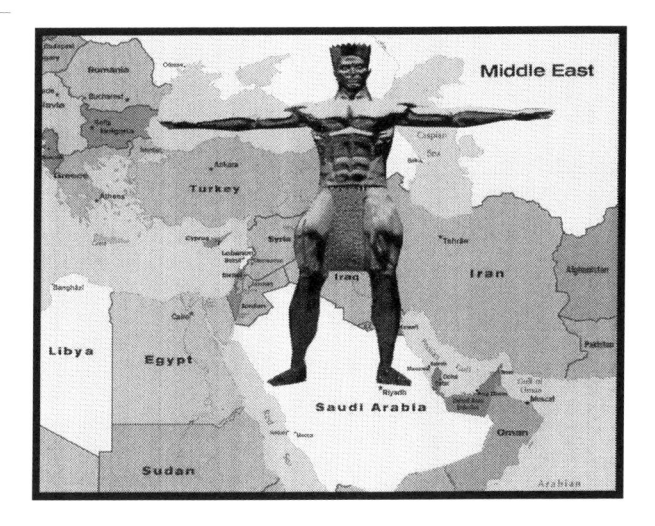

As we look at this picture, there is something interesting that we should know about the first three kingdoms. Each of the first three kingdoms depicted had their capitals in the ancient city of Babylon. Ancient Babylon was located in present day Iraq.

Therefore, the location of the statue whose arms stretched from Greece to India was always located in what is now Iraq. This leaves us with the question of where will the statue's fourth kingdom appear?

Unless someone moves the statue, it would appear that the fourth kingdom will appear centered in Iraq.

However, to answer the question, where will the fourth kingdom arise, we would be wise to consult Scripture. Because, if we have a biblical question, we should let Yahweh do the talking. As good Bible students say, "Let Scripture interpret Scripture."

Therefore our question about the statue is the following: Do the historical territories depicted by the statue indicate the geographical territory that will be controlled by the Fourth Kingdom as described in Daniel 2?

There is a considerable amount of biblical prophecy which identifies the location of the fourth kingdom, the future kingdom of the beast known as the Antichrist. Therefore, I will devote an additional chapter to this topic. We will biblically examine the Antichrist and where the Kingdom of the Antichrist will arise in the chapter titled More about Antichrist.

Each of Daniel's prophecies concerns the Time of the End, the time that leads to the Second Coming of the Messiah and the Kingdom of Yahweh on earth. Each of Daniel's prophecies also provides additional information about the future kingdom of the Antichrist.

Chapter 3

Kingdom with Ten Kings

> "The ten horns are ten kings who will come from this kingdom. After them another king will arise, different from the earlier ones; he will subdue three kings."
>
> **Daniel 7:24**

Daniel's second prophecy provides additional information about the coming kingdom of the Antichrist. Daniel himself received the dream and again Yahweh revealed the meaning of the dream. Daniel wrote down the dream and it is recorded in Daniel 7:1-16.

Daniel's dream contains several descriptions that connect with Revelation's prophetic description about the Antichrist and his kingdom. Let's compare a few of these descriptions so that we see the similarity.

Daniel and Revelation concerning the "sea."

> "In my vision at night I looked, and there before me were the four winds of heaven churning up the great sea." Daniel 7:2)

"And the dragon stood on the shore of the sea. And I saw a beast coming out of the sea." (Revelation 13:1)

Daniel and Revelation concerning the beasts.

"The first was **like a lion…** a second beast, which looked **like a bear…** another beast, one that looked **like a leopard" (Daniel 7:4-6)**

"The beast I saw **resembled a leopard**, but had feet **like those of a bear** and a mouth **like that of a lion.**" (Revelation 13:2)

Daniel and Revelation: the "10 horns and 7 heads"

"It was different from all the former beasts, and **it had ten horns.** While I was thinking about the horns, there before me was another horn, a little one, which came up among them; and **three of the first horns were uprooted.**" (Daniel 7:7-8)

The "beast coming out of the sea. He had **ten horns and seven heads**, with ten crowns on his horns." (Revelation 13:1)

These similarities between Daniel and Revelation reveal several things about the Antichrist and his kingdom. In prophecy a reference to "sea" often symbolizes peoples or nations and the first three beasts symbolize the first three kingdoms; lion (Babylon), bear (Media-Persia) and leopard (Greece). These similarities connect the fourth kingdom, the future kingdom of the Antichrist, with the first three kingdoms.

The prophecy indicates that the Antichrist will rise to world power out of the people of these ancient kingdoms of Babylon, Media-Persia and Greece. The reference to "ten horns and seven heads" indicates how the fourth kingdom will develop into the kingdom of the Antichrist.

The Kingdom then the Antichrist

> "It was different from all the former beasts, and **it had ten horns.** While I was thinking about the horns, there before me was another horn, a little one, which came up among them; and **three of the first horns were uprooted.**" (Daniel 7:7-8)

The fourth kingdom will start with 10 kings (horns) and then the Antichrist (a little horn) will arise to power among them. When the little horn takes his place, he will replace one of the original 10 leaders. The kingdom will still have 10 kings. According to Revelation, the Antichrist and the kingdom of 10 will be responsible for the destruction of Mystery Babylon the Great, by fire in one day and one hour.

> "**The beast (Antichrist) and the ten horns** you saw will hate the prostitute (Babylon the Great). They **will bring her to ruin** and leave her naked; they will eat her flesh **and burn her with fire.**" (Revelation 17:16)

Later after the destruction of "Babylon the Great" the kingdom will not remain united as we see described in this prophecy and as we saw in Daniel's statue prophecy.

> "And just as you saw the iron mixed with baked clay, so the people will be a mixture and will not remain united." (Daniel 2:43)

After the destruction of "Mystery Babylon the Great," three of the original 10 kings will be "uprooted" and "subdued." That is when the fourth kingdom of 10 nations will become the kingdom with "**ten horns and seven heads**" just as we saw in our comparison between Daniel and Revelation earlier.

First Tribulation then Second Coming

Daniel's dream about the fourth kingdom also reveals that at the time of the fourth kingdom, the Antichrist will be destroyed and thrown into the blazing fire. This will happen as we saw in Daniel 7, when "**one like a son of man, coming with the clouds ... and his kingdom is one that will never be destroyed.**"

Daniel was very troubled by his dream and asked the Lord to tell him about the fourth kingdom. This is the explanation that Daniel received:

> "The fourth beast is a fourth kingdom that will appear on earth. It will be different from all the other kingdoms and will devour the whole earth, trampling it down and crushing it. **The ten horns are ten kings who will come from this kingdom. After them another king will arise, different from the earlier ones; he will subdue three kings.**" (Daniel 7:23-24)

Just as we saw in the dream, Yahweh's explanation confirms how the fourth kingdom will form and become the kingdom of the Antichrist. In the explanation God tells Daniel about the final three and a half years of persecution of the saints which Christ referred to as the "Great Tribulation," in Matthew 24:21.

> "He will speak against the Most High and oppress his saints and try to change the set times and the laws. **The saints will be handed over to him for a time, times and half a time** [3 ½ years]. But the court will sit, and his power will be taken away and completely destroyed forever. Then the sovereignty, power and greatness of the kingdoms under the whole heaven will be handed over to the saints, the people of **the Most High. His kingdom will be an everlasting kingdom**, and all rulers will worship and obey him." (Daniel 7:25-27)

Finally, God reveals to Daniel, again as He did in Daniel's statue prophecy, that the Most High will defeat the Beast kingdom and deliver His kingdom to the saints forever.

What we know about the four beast kingdoms:

- The first three were Babylon (lion), Media-Persia (bear) and Greece (leopard).
- The fourth kingdom will begin with 10 kings.
- Then another king will rise among them.
- The fourth kingdom will devour the whole earth.

- The Antichrist will subdue 3 of the original kings.
- The fourth kingdom will be destroyed by return of the Messiah when He sets up His eternal kingdom.

Chapter 4

When Rebels become Terrorists

> "In the latter part of their reign, when rebels have become completely wicked, a stern-faced king, a master of intrigue, will arise."
>
> **Daniel 8:23**

This is Daniel's third prophecy concerning the kingdom of the Antichrist. This prophecy builds on the previous two prophecies, in Daniel 2 and 7, which we have already examined.

Media-Persia and Greece

In this prophecy Yahweh identified the second and third kingdoms by name.

> "The two-horned ram that you saw represents the kings of Media and Persia. The shaggy goat is the king of Greece." (Daniel 8:20-21)

Now, let's see what else we can learn about the Antichrist and our future.

As we read this prophecy about the Kingdom of Media-Persia and how it was defeated by Alexander the Great of Greece, remember this prophecy was given before these events had happened.

> "I watched the ram (Media-Persia) as he charged toward the west and the north and the south. No animal could stand against him, and none could rescue from his power. He did as he pleased and became great. As I was thinking about this, suddenly a goat (Greece) with a prominent horn between his eyes came from the west, **crossing the whole earth without touching the ground.**" Daniel 8:4-5)

I should point out that all fulfilled prophecies have always been fulfilled literally and precisely as they were described in Scripture.

Let's look at an example of fulfilled prophecy to see just how literal and precise Bible prophecy is.

Without Touching the Ground

Here is a little known fact regarding biblical prophecy that you can use to impress your friends.

In Daniel's chapter 8 prophecy we find recorded a prophetic vision and a divine interpretation which includes precise details regarding the rise and fall of several Middle-eastern kings and kingdoms. Daniel was told that the kings of Media and Persia would defeat the King of Babylon. Then a great king from Greece (Alexander the Great) would conquer the kings of Media and Persia.

In this vision Daniel was told that the "goat with a prominent horn came from the west, crossing the whole earth **without touching the ground**" (Daniel 8:5).

This prophecy is a good example of the literal accuracy and precision of God's prophetic Word.

First, the prophecy specifically gave the names of the future Middle-eastern kingdoms of Media-Persia and Greece years before they came to power.

Second, Daniel's prophecy above says something very unusual, in the English translation, which turns out to be precisely and literally accurate.

It says that "a prominent horn" which was Alexander the Great, "came from the west, crossing the whole earth" which he did. But then it says that he (Alexander) did this "without touching the ground." How can that be? There were no airplanes at the time of Alexander the Great.

Note: When you check your Bible translations on this passage, most English translations use "ground" when translating the original Hebrew word "'erets." 'Erets can mean either ground or land. In some of Daniel's other prophecies he uses "'erets" when referring to the land of Israel, the Beautiful Land, see Daniel 11:16, 41. Therefore, "'erets" in this context should be translated land as in the Beautiful Land a.k.a. the Promised Land.

Alexander was Great

In history, here is what happened when Alexander the Great left Greece and was sweeping across the known world conquering every country in his path. He came to the Promised "Land" of Israel. There in Jerusalem a Jewish priest explained to Alexander this prophecy recorded in Daniel which foretold of a great king from Greece.

> Josephus recorded that when Alexander arrived to attack Jerusalem the High Priest showed him a copy of the book of Daniel. The book of Daniel showed him that a great Greek king should destroy the empire of the Persians; he supposed that he was that person. He was so impressed by this that instead of destroying Jerusalem he entered the city peaceably and worshiped at the Temple.[1]

---

[1] http://otstory.wordpress.com/2008/08/03/why-did-alexander-the-great-like-the-book-of-daniel/

Alexander, believing that this prophecy was about him, was so pleased that he continued on with his conquests toward Egypt without conquering the land of Israel.

Therefore, as the prophecy states Alexander "came from the west, crossing the whole earth without touching the land [Promised Land]." The history of Alexander the Great became the precise literal fulfillment of Daniel's prophecy.

Too bad so many translators missed this fact in their translations. The Word of God is all true, but occasionally the translators miss the best way to translate the Hebrew and Greek into English. However, don't be too concerned because all the major translations are fine and you can count on them. However, there are students who have to know what the Word says, exactly. For them it is good that we have the original languages to refer to.

Let's press on and look at the rest of the prophecy piece by piece. After Alexander the Great died his kingdom was divided among his four prominent generals.

> "The goat became very great (Alexander the Great), but at the height of his power his large horn was broken off, and in its place four prominent horns (four generals) grew up toward the four winds of heaven. Out of one of them came another horn, which started small but grew in power to the south and to the east and toward the Beautiful Land." Daniel 8:8-9)

It will be out of one of the four parts of Alexander's divided empire that the future kingdom of the Antichrist will arise to world dominance.

In this next piece of the prophecy the beast we know as the Antichrist will take away the daily sacrifice and set himself up in God's temple and proclaims himself to be God.

> "It [beast] set itself up to be as great as the Prince of the host [God]; it took away the daily sacrifice from him, and the place of his sanctuary was brought low. Because of rebellion, the host of the saints and the daily sacrifice were given over to it. It prospered in everything it did, and truth was thrown to the ground." (Daniel 8:11-12)

Next the prophecy indicates that the Kingdom of the Antichrist will arise out of Alexander the Great's Kingdom which was divided into four parts by his generals following his death.

> "The four horns (generals), that replaced the one that was broken off (Alexander), represent four kingdoms that will emerge from his nation but will not have the same power." (Daniel 8:22)

When Antichrist Arises

Then at the appointed time in the near future, when rebels have become completely wicked, the Antichrist will arise from one of the parts of Alexander's kingdom. Today it seems that rebels have already become completely wicked, when they blow up buses filled with women and children. Today, rebels are often called terrorists. In the verse below the Antichrist is called a stern-faced king, a master of intrigue.

> "In the latter part of their reign, **when rebels have become completely wicked**, a stern-faced king, a master of intrigue, will arise." (Daniel 8:23)

Last Man Standing

This next verse says something very revealing. It says that the Antichrist will be become very strong because of the power of someone else. In Daniel's time they did not refer to powerful nations as superpowers, they would call them the "mighty men" or the "mightiest fortresses."

Since he is a master of intrigue, perhaps the Antichrist convinces one superpower to attack another superpower and then when the superpowers destroy each other, the Antichrist would become very powerful.

Today, if two or three superpowers were to fight they could engage in thermo-nuclear war. If that were the case no superpower would emerge the victor. But the Antichrist could be the last man standing and become very strong indeed.

This passage also confirms that we are talking about the Antichrist because it is the Antichrist who is responsible for the Great Tribulation which is the time when the saints will be nearly destroyed.

> "**He will become very strong, but not by his own power**. He will cause astounding devastation and will succeed in whatever he does. He will destroy the mighty men and the holy people." (Daniel 8:24)

The above verse when considered in connection with other Time of the End prophecies indicates just how this prophecy will be fulfilled. In the very near future the U.S.A. will no longer be the only Superpower in the world. Then the Antichrist will persuade Russia and possibly China to attack the U.S.A. When this happens the U.S.A. would be defeated and Russia and China would be severely damaged. Then the Antichrist will be the last man standing and become very strong.

Not only is the Antichrist a master of intrigue, but he is also deceitful and he will destroy many. But that is not the end of the prophecy.

Destroyed by God

After the Antichrist takes his stand against God at the "abomination that causes desolation" when he proclaims that he is God, in the temple of God, the Antichrist will be destroyed by God when the Messiah returns.

> "He (Antichrist) will cause deceit to prosper, and he will consider himself superior. When they feel secure, **he will destroy many and take his stand against the Prince of princes**. Yet he will be destroyed, but not by human power." (Daniel 8:25)

I will cover the "abomination that causes desolation" in some detail in the next chapter. Then you will see exactly what this prophecy is saying, when it says "he will destroy many and take his stand against the Prince of princes."

In the last two verses we were told that, when the Antichrist arises, he will "succeed in whatever he does" and "cause deceit to prosper, and he will consider himself superior." Never-the-less, as we have already seen in Daniel's first three prophecies, the Antichrist will ultimately be destroyed by the Messiah when He returns and establishes the eternal Kingdom on earth.

What we know about the Antichrist:

- He will arise when "rebels have become" terrorists.
- He will become strong by someone else's power.
- He will cause astounding devastation.
- He will stand against the Messiah, called Christ.
- He will destroy the mighty men and the holy people.
- He will be destroyed by Yahweh.

Chapter 5

First Antichrist Wars

> "He will attack the mightiest fortresses with the help of a foreign god and will greatly honor those who acknowledge him. He will make them rulers over many people and will distribute the land at a price."
>
> **Daniel 11:39**

Like each of Daniel's earlier prophecies, Daniel 11 includes things that happened in the past as well as what will happen in the future, when the Antichrist is arising to world power.

As far as I can tell, everything that Daniel prophesied in chapter 11 up through verse 35 has been fulfilled and recorded in history. There are differences of opinion regarding where in the prophecy history stops and the future begins. However, most seem to agree that the first 35 verses are fulfilled prophecy. I will be starting with verse 35 and explain what I see from there through the balance of the chapter and the activities of the Antichrist.

For those who would like to read an historical summary of Daniel 11:1-35, I will recommend "**Daniel 11a - History Leads to the Final Crisis verses 1-35.**"[2] There are many other accounts available online.

[2] http://www.bibleexplained.com/prophets/daniel/da11.htm

Antiochus Epiphanes the ruler over the Jews from **175-164 B.C.** seems to have fulfilled much of what is written during the time of verses 30 through 35. He and his army desecrated the temple and abolished the daily sacrifice. He also took many actions against Jerusalem, the Temple and the Jewish people.

The reason not everyone agrees as to when history stops and the future begins in this prophecy is because future prophecy about "the abomination that causes desolation" seems very similar to these five verses. One reason I believe we should still keep these verses in mind is because verse 31 indicates that this is "the abomination that causes desolation." In my mind Antiochus Epiphanes and his forces set up "an" abomination, he did not set up "the" abomination. The "abomination that causes desolation" (Matthew 24:15 and Daniel 9:27) will not happen until the Antichrist does what apostle Paul describes below:

> "He (Antichrist) will oppose and will exalt himself over everything that is called God or is worshiped, so that he sets himself up in God's temple, proclaiming himself to be God." (2 Thessalonians 2:4)

Now, let's take a quick look at the verses in question and then we will move on to the prophecy about our future.

Antiochus Epiphanes or Antichrist?

"His armed forces will rise up to desecrate the temple fortress and will abolish the daily sacrifice. Then they will set up the abomination that causes desolation. With flattery he will corrupt those who have violated the covenant, but the people who know their God will firmly resist him. Those who are wise will instruct many, though for a time they will fall by the sword or be burned or captured or plundered. When they fall, they will receive a little help, and many who are not sincere will join them. Some of the wise will stumble, so that they may be refined, purified and made spotless until the time of the end, for it will still come at the appointed time." (Daniel 11:31-35)

The last sentence in the above verse says, "the time of the end will still come at the appointed time." I believe we are now in that Time, the time Christ said would last less than a generation, see Matthew 24:33-34. So let's see what Daniel says will soon be taking place.

The rest of Daniel 11's prophecy describes the king we know as the Antichrist and the things that will happen as he rises to power. The "he" in this part of the prophecy is always speaking of the Antichrist. Now, let's have Daniel tell us about this beast king known as the Antichrist and his rise to world domination. You will see numbers, which I have inserted, as you read the prophecy. These numbers mark four observations which I will refer to shortly.

"The king will do as he pleases. **He will exalt and magnify himself above every god** and will say unheard-of things against the God of gods. (**1** He will be successful until the time of wrath is completed,) for what has been determined must take place. (**2** He will show no regard for the gods of his fathers or for the one desired by women, nor will he regard any god,) but (**3** will exalt himself above them all.) Instead of them, (**4** he will honor a god of fortresses;) a god unknown to his fathers he will honor with gold and silver, with precious stones and costly gifts." (Daniel 11:36-38)

We can be very certain that this king is the Antichrist because the apostle Paul used these same words to describe him below:

"He (Antichrist) will oppose and will exalt himself over everything that is called God or is worshiped, so that he sets himself up in God's temple, proclaiming himself to be God." (2 Thessalonians 2:4)

There are a few other observations that I believe we should consider about the Antichrist:

1. "He will be successful until the time of wrath is completed," at Messiah's return.

2. It appears that he will change from old religious beliefs which would mean no Islam, no Judaism and no Christianity. "He will show no regard for the gods of his fathers (Islam) or for the one desired by women (Christ)."

3. He will exalt himself and proclaim that he is God.

4. He will honor military might, "he will honor a god of fortresses."

This fourth point is important to keep in mind because from everything that prophecy tells us, the Antichrist will be a warrior king – not the peace maker that many false prophecy teachers have imagined.

Yahweh has guided me to point out the truth of Scripture not spend my time bashing the false teachers and prophets that are prevalent today.

Prophecy itself warns us against these popular teachings. Here is what Yahweh and Christ say about the religious teachers at the Time of the End:

> "Son of man, prophesy against the prophets of Israel who are now prophesying. Say to **those who prophesy out of their own imagination: 'Hear the word of Yahweh!'**" (Ezekiel 13:2)

Those who prophecy out of their own imaginations are going beyond what is written in Scripture, proclaiming things that God never said, even though Yahweh warned them not to, as He says below.

> "**Do not go beyond what is written**. Then you will not take pride in one man over against another." (1 Corinthians 4:6)

Christ also warned us that this false teaching would happen in the household of God.

> "Watch out that no one deceives you. For **many will come in my name… and will deceive many**." (Matthew 24:4-5)

With that said, let's move on to see what Daniel indicates will happen as the Antichrist rises to world power. Once again God tells Daniel that the Antichrist will have help in his rise to world domination. Just like in Daniel 8, in Daniel 11 we're told something very similar. Let compare the two to see how God says the Antichrist is successful in becoming very strong.

> "**He will become very strong, but not by his own power**. He will cause astounding devastation and will succeed in whatever he does. **He will destroy the mighty men** and the holy people." (Daniel 8:24)

> "**He (Antichrist) will attack the mightiest fortresses with the help of a foreign god (foreign power)** and will greatly honor those who acknowledge him. He will make them rulers over many people and will distribute the land at a price." (Daniel 11:39)

Something New

A few years ago Yahweh showed me something that I had never seen, even though I had read and studied these prophecies hundreds of times. As a matter of fact I am not aware of anyone else who has seen this aspect of Daniel's prophecies. As far as I know this is a completely new revelation which I received from Yahweh, the Holy Spirit.

There were a couple of other things in the Word that helped me see what I am about to show you. The first of which was something that Yahweh had been teaching me for several years which had to do with the Seals of Revelation. Yahweh has shown me how the Seals of Revelation are key to understanding the Time of the End.

Because of their importance to our discussion concerning the Antichrist, I will be presenting 'The Seals of Revelations' in relation to the Antichrist in subsequent chapters.

Another thing that helped me see what I am going show you is Daniel 7's prophecy about the rise of the Antichrist. First the kingdom of 10 kings will come together, then the Antichrist would join them before he will subdue 3 of the original kings.

> "The ten horns are ten kings who will come from this kingdom. After them another king will arise, different from the earlier ones; **he will subdue three kings.**" (Daniel 7:23-24)

With this in mind, I will show to you who the 3 kings are that will be subdued by the Antichrist and when it will happen.

1. **Who are the three subdued?**

2. **When will they be subdued?**

Now, let's examine Daniel's prophecy in order to answer these two questions. I will **bolden** portions of the Prophecy for emphasis. First, who are the three that will be subdued by the Antichrist?

> "**At the time of the end** the king of the South will engage him (Antichrist) in battle, and the king of the North will storm out against him with chariots and cavalry and a great fleet of ships. He will invade many countries and sweep through them like a flood. He will also invade the Beautiful Land. Many countries will fall, but Edom, Moab and the leaders of Ammon will be delivered from his hand. He will extend his power over many countries; Egypt will not escape. **He (Antichrist) will gain control** of the treasures of gold and silver and all the riches **of Egypt, with the Libyans and Nubians (Sudan) in submission.**" (Daniel 11:40-43)

The Nubians were an ancient tribe of people who today are located in Sudan, just to the south of Egypt.

With this information we can identify three of the ten kings who initially form the kings of Daniel 7.

1. **Who are the three subdued?**

   - Egypt
   - Libya
   - Sudan

In the Daniel 2 prophecy about the statue we were told that the people of the fourth kingdom would not remain united. Now, with the information from Daniel 7 and 11 we see how that union is broken. When Egypt, Libya and Sudan attack the Antichrist, they are subdued.

Now, the second question:

2. **When will they be subdued?**

In verses 40-43 above we saw the events which lead to the three kings being subdued. So what happens before these events? Before the three are subdued,

> "He (Antichrist) will attack the mightiest fortresses with the help of a foreign god." (Daniel 11:39)

Therefore, it appears that the three will be subdued after the superpowers are attacked and "Mystery Babylon the Great" is destroyed. This is also confirmed by what we read in Revelation 17. In Revelation 17 we are told that all ten kings hate the prostitute "Babylon the Great" (Revelation 17:5) and bring her to ruin by fire.

> "**The beast (Antichrist) and the ten horns** you saw will hate the prostitute. They will bring her to ruin and leave her naked; they will eat her flesh and burn her with fire." (Revelation 17:16)

Therefore, the three will be subdued after "Babylon the Great" is destroyed.

Before I finish this prophecy, I would like to go back and show you something else that happens when Egypt attacks the Antichrist. Once again I will **bolden** portions of the prophecy for emphasis.

> "At the time of the end the king of the South will engage him (Antichrist) in battle ... He (Antichrist) will invade many countries and sweep through them like a flood. **(1) He will also invade the Beautiful Land**. ... He will gain control of the treasures of gold and silver and all the riches of Egypt, with the Libyans and Nubians (Sudan) in submission." (Daniel 11:40-43)

It appears from prophecy that there will be three times that the Antichrist invades Israel.

1. On this the first occasion, the Antichrist will confirm a covenant. This covenant will have been a treaty previously made by others.

2. Three and a half years later he will return with his army, enter the temple of Yahweh and proclaim that he is God in what is called the "abomination that causes desolation."

3. Finally, there will be a third time. This is when the Antichrist and the nations will gather at Armageddon north of Jerusalem, come down the Valley of Jehoshaphat to attack Jerusalem and the Messiah who will have already returned.

One of the reasons I believe it will happen this way is because each of these occasions is considered a birth-pain and corresponds to the Seals of Revelation which I will address in chapter nine.

The prophecy describes the second time the Antichrist invades Israel. This time he sets himself up in **the temple on the Holy Mount Zion** and proclaims himself to be God.

Finally, about three and a half years later the Antichrist will come to his end at the hands of the returning Messiah.

Here is how the prophecy reads:

> "But reports from the east and the north will alarm him, and he will set out in a great rage to destroy and annihilate many. **(2) He will pitch his royal tents between the seas at the beautiful holy mountain**. **(3) Yet he will come to his end,** and no one will help him." (Daniel 11:44-45)

We have examined five of Daniel's six prophecies and one remains. Each of Daniel's prophecies provides details to the Time of the End, all of which will help Yahweh's people understand this very dangerous and critical time. The Time of the End leads up to the return of the Messiah the King, when He will establish His kingdom on earth.

What we know about the Antichrist:

- He will be a Warrior King.
- He will attack the Superpowers
- He will be attacked by Egypt, Libya and Sudan.
- He will subdue Egypt, Libya and Sudan
- He will invade Israel.
- He will set himself up on Mount Zion.
- He will come to his end.

Chapter 6

Antichrist's Last 7 Years

> "He will confirm a covenant with many for one 'seven.' In the middle of the 'seven' he will put an end to sacrifice and offering. And at the temple he will set up an abomination that causes desolation, until the end that is decreed is poured out on him."
>
> Daniel 9:27

In Daniel chapter nine is one of the most amazing prophecies in the Bible. Because of its importance to End Time prophecy I am going to cover it in some detail. However, only the last couple of verses of the Daniel 9 prophecy directly relate to the Antichrist.

This prophecy we will refer to as Daniel's "Seventy Sevens" prophecy. This prophecy provides specific information which enables us to determine the exact time of the First Coming of Christ. This same prophecy also provides several details describing key events of the last seven years of Daniel's prophecy, which we will call Daniel's 70th 'seven'.

First we will examine this prophecy regarding the First Coming of Christ and then we will study the last seven-years concerning the Antichrist, the leader who will come.

At the time Darius ruled from Babylon, Daniel came to understand from the prophecy of Jeremiah 25:11 that the desolation of Jerusalem would last seventy years. When Daniel realized the desolation of Jerusalem was coming to a close he began to seek Yahweh in prayer and petition concerning the restoration of Jerusalem and the temple. While Daniel was praying he received the "Seventy Sevens" prophecy which he was told to consider and understand.

The "Seventy Sevens" prophecy consists of four-verses which have astounded scholars and students for centuries. So accurate are the details of this prophecy that skeptics have insisted that the book of Daniel must have been written after Christ's First Coming. However, since the discoveries of the Dead Sea Scrolls in Qumran between 1948 and 1952, the skeptics have been relatively quiet on this topic.

The Dead Sea Scrolls discoveries included the book of Daniel, and it has been determined that these scrolls predated Christ's First Coming by at least 200 years. Therefore, these discoveries provided archeological evidence confirming that the prophecies of Daniel predated Christ's First Coming.

Know and Understand

Now let's turn to Daniel's "Seventy Sevens" prophecy. When Daniel was given this prophecy he was commanded twice to know and understand the vision and prophecy.

>"**Therefore, consider the message and understand the vision.**" (Daniel 9:23)

>"**Know and understand this**" (Daniel 9:25)

The commands to understand this prophecy were later repeated by Christ when He gave His followers a similar command saying, "**let the reader understand,**" in Matthew 24:15.

Therefore, in case we might have missed the importance of this prophecy, Yahweh commanded His people to know and understand this prophecy no less than three times in His Word. Needless to say, this prophecy is important.

Now, as we consider this vision we find that the first verse establishes the time frame of this prophecy.

>"Seventy 'sevens' [shabuwa] are decreed for your people and your holy city to finish transgression, to put an end to sin, to atone for wickedness, to bring in everlasting righteousness, to seal up vision and prophecy and to anoint the most holy." (Daniel 9:24)

In Hebrew 'shabuwa' is translated "sevens." Shabuwa means sevened, seven or a week."[1] The fulfillment of the first part of this prophecy in history has verified that the meaning of shabuwa, here, means seven years. As we will shortly see the first sixty-nine of the "seventy sevens" have been fulfilled exactly as prophesied. So, we know with certainty that shabuwa in Daniel's "Seventy Sevens" prophecy means seven years and "seventy sevens" equals 490 years.

Therefore, 490 years are decreed for "your people and your holy city" Jerusalem to:

1. Finish transgression
2. End sin
3. Atone for wickedness
4. Bring in everlasting righteousness
5. Seal up vision and prophecy
6. Anoint the most holy

These six items list what the prophecy says will be accomplished for the people of Yahweh and the holy city (Jerusalem) at the conclusion of the 490 years.

---

[1] Strong's Concordance transliterated Hebrew and Greek – *shabuwa,* H7620

While we could debate whether or not Christ accomplished some of these things on the cross, it is evident that not everything has been fulfilled at the present time. For example, regarding the sealing up of prophecy, Scripture reveals that prophecy will continue to the very end of the age, because it is written that two witnesses will prophesy for 1,260 days, see Revelation 11:3. Therefore, since prophecy has not yet been sealed up, the final fulfillment of Daniel's "Seventy Sevens" is still in the future. And even though Christ paid the atonement price for sin, we still see that sin is present and everlasting righteousness has not yet been achieved.

Daniel 9:24 indicates that after 490 years, Yahweh will restore everything to His people and His holy city Jerusalem.

From the decree - March 14, 445 BC

As we have seen in Daniel 9:25, Yahweh says that we are to "know and understand." Because with this prophecy the people of Yahweh would be able determine the exact time of the First Coming of the Messiah. We have already seen from Jesus' statements to the Jewish leaders, in Luke 19:44 that He expected them to have known the time of His First Coming.

We already know that the entire prophecy is 490 years in duration. Therefore, we now need to know when the 490 years begins. Daniel provides the answer in this verse.

> "Know and understand this: From the issuing of the decree to restore and rebuild Jerusalem until the Anointed One [Messiah], the ruler [King], comes, there will be seven 'sevens,' and sixty-two 'sevens.' It will be rebuilt with streets and a trench, but in times of trouble." (Daniel 9:25)

Daniel tells us that there will be a decree to restore and rebuild Jerusalem. Also implied in the rebuilding of Jerusalem is the rebuilding of the temple. We know this because Daniel was seeking Yahweh in prayer for the restoration of Jerusalem and the temple [2] and because when the decree was issued it included the city of Jerusalem and the temple.

There has, however, been debate over the years about which decree started the timing for this prophecy. There were a total of four decrees that were issued to rebuild the temple. The first three decrees called for the rebuilding of only the temple and they are recorded in the book of Ezra.

In Ezra 1:1-4 (Cyrus mentions only the temple); Ezra 6:1-12 (mentions the decree to rebuild the temple issued by Darius Hystaspis); and Ezra 7:11-26 (records the third decree, issued by Artaxerxes Lonimanus during the seventh year of his reign). Each of these first three decrees called for the rebuilding of the temple, the rebuilding of Jerusalem was not included in any of these first three decrees.

---

[2] Daniel 9:17-18

However, there was a fourth decree which did call for the rebuilding of Jerusalem. This decree, which is recorded in Nehemiah 2:5-18, allows us to identify the exact date when this prophecy of the "seventy sevens" begins.

This decree was made on March 14, 445 BC.[3]

Remember, from verse twenty-six, from the time of the decree to restore and rebuild Jerusalem there will be "seven sevens" and "sixty-two sevens" or sixty-nine "sevens" (483 years) until "the anointed one, the ruler" comes.

So that we understand clearly who this is about let's look at the Hebrew words for "the anointed one the ruler." "The Hebrew word mashiyach"[4] means, "anointed one" and nagiyd[5] means "ruler, prince or leader." The Hebrew word mashiyach is where we get the title Messiah. Nagiyd is the title which was used to refer to Saul the first King of Israel, in Samuel 9:16.

---

[3] Sir Robert Anderson, The Coming Prince, 1895 - Kregel Classics 1957

[4] Strong's Concordance transliterated Hebrew – *mashiyach*, H4899

[5] Strong's Concordance transliterated Hebrew – *nagiyd*, H5057

Therefore, it would also be correct to translate "mashiyach nagiyd" as "Messiah the King." If we where to put "Messiah the King" into New Testament terms we would say "Christ the King." Therefore, this verse tells us that from the decree until Christ the King comes there will be 483 years.

To understand the time period of this prophecy we will refer to the work of Sir Robert Anderson who first published his classic study on the interpretation of Daniel's prophecy, titled the 'The Coming Prince' in 1895.[6] In his research Anderson demonstrated that the time from the decree in March 14, 445 BC to April 6, 32 AD was exactly 483 years to the day. The calculation was made using the Jewish calendar which contains 360 days. The scholarship of his work was so sound that his book continues to be an authoritative work and is still being reprinted today.

To the Messiah the King - April 6, 32 AD

At the time of the Messiah's First Advent some of the Jewish people understood that Daniel's prophecy would find its fulfillment with the coming of the Messiah the King. Scripture was clear that the Messiah would reign over the people of the earth from David's throne at the restoration of all things. For example:

---

[6] Sir Robert Anderson, The Coming Prince, 1895 - Kregel Classics 1957

> "Of the increase of his government and peace there will be no end. He will reign on David's throne and over his kingdom, establishing and upholding it with justice and righteousness from that time on and forever." (Isaiah 9:7)

They also knew that the reign of the Messiah would be a time of righteousness and all nations of the earth would live in peace. That is what the Jewish people were waiting for as they looked forward to the coming of the Messiah the King. Because of the details of Daniel's prophecy they also had a very good idea when the Messiah was to be expected. That is very likely why we find in the Gospels that the whole nation of Israel was looking for the Messiah at the very time of His First Advent. They knew, just as we know today, that the prophecies of Scripture cannot be broken and all Scripture must be fulfilled as it is written. The Messiah was coming to fulfill prophecy at the appointed time. So how do we know that April 6, 32 AD was the correct time for the Messiah's coming? Good question! How does the Bible answer this question? April 6, 32 AD is the date Jesus rode the colt of a donkey into Jerusalem.

The First Coming

From the beginning, before His First Advent, the Messiah was destined to be King. However, the timing of His coming as King could only be at the appointed time as foretold by the prophets. As we read through the Gospels we find times when the people wanted to take Jesus and make Him King, but He would not allow it. Then one day He began to make specific arrangements to fulfill the timing of the prophets, just as written. Both King David in Psalm 118 and Zechariah in chapter 9 prophesied of the coming Messiah, allowing us to determine the exact circumstances that would take place at the appointed time of the Messiah's First Coming.

Look at the picture David portrays in Psalm 118. He writes an account of the Lord's entry into the holy city of Jerusalem complete with festival procession, boughs being waved and shouts of "save us." David even seems to prophesy the sacrifice that would follow when he writes "to the horns of the altar." This indicates that the Messiah was going to make a sacrifice. It is at "the horns of the altar" where the atonement for sin is made.

> "This is the day Yahweh has made; let us rejoice and be glad in it. O Yahweh, save us; O Yahweh, grant us success. **Blessed is he who comes in the name of Yahweh**. From the house of Yahweh we bless you. Yahweh is God, and he has made his light shine upon us. **With boughs in hand**, join in the festal procession up **to the horns of the altar**." (Psalm 118:24-27)

This is an amazingly descriptive prophecy showing the Messiah coming to the house of the Lord in Jerusalem and His subsequent sacrifice. This and several other prophecies substantiate that this was the appointed time for the coming of the Messiah the King.

Zechariah also prophesied about the coming King, saying He would enter Jerusalem riding on the colt of a donkey. When we compare these prophecies with the record of their fulfillment, there can be no doubt that this is the coming of Messiah, as foretold in Daniel 9:25.

> "Rejoice greatly, O Daughter of Zion! Shout, Daughter of Jerusalem! **See, your king comes to you,** righteous and having salvation, gentle and riding on a donkey, on a colt, the foal of a donkey." (Zechariah 9:9)

The crowds in Jerusalem shouted, "Hosanna to the Son of David!" Hosanna means save and the "Son of David" is a reference to the Messiah. In Psalm 118:25 there is a festival procession with people shouting "save us; O Yahweh." Compare these passages and see the fulfillment that marked the exact time of Daniel 9:25. The Messiah offered Himself as King when He entered Jerusalem on April 6, 32 AD.

This is how the prophesied event is recorded in the Gospel of Matthew.

> **"This took place to fulfill what was spoken through the prophet: 'Say to the Daughter of Zion, 'See, your king comes to you, gentle and riding on a donkey, on a colt, the foal of a donkey'**… They brought the donkey and the colt, placed their cloaks on them, and Jesus sat on them. A very large crowd spread their cloaks on the road, while others cut branches from the trees and spread them on the road. The crowds that went ahead of him and those that followed shouted, 'Hosanna to the Son of David!' 'Blessed is he who comes in the name of the Lord!' 'Hosanna in the highest!' When Jesus entered Jerusalem, the whole city was stirred and asked, 'Who is this?'" (Matthew 21:4-10)

If only they had known the time of His coming and had recognized the Messiah the King! Jesus seems to confirm that this was the exact day which had been prophesied, when He said, as He was approaching Jerusalem, "If you, even you, had only known **on this day** what would bring you peace--but now it is hidden from your eyes." (Luke 19:42)

Jesus makes a Covenant by Sacrifice

After Jesus rode into Jerusalem and offered himself as the Messiah the King, Daniel says that the Messiah would be **cut off**.

> "After the sixty-two 'sevens,' the Anointed One will be **cut off** [karath] and will have nothing." (Daniel 9:26)

When Daniel writes that after the "sixty-two sevens" which follows the "seven sevens" in Daniel 9:25, he is saying that after the "sixty-nine sevens" the Messiah will be cut off. Therefore, after Jesus' coming on April 6, 32 AD, Daniel tells us that the Messiah the King will be cut off. This corresponds exactly to the Gospel account which indicates that Jesus went to the cross and was crucified just days after his triumphal entry into Jerusalem.

To understand what is being prophesied, it's helpful to understand what is meant by the term "cut off." Almost every English Bible translation of Daniel 9:26 render the Hebrew word 'karath' as "cut off." Since the term "cut off" seems a bit obscure, we might ask what is the meaning of the word 'karath'? According to Strong's Concordance, "karath means to make a covenant (i.e. make an alliance or bargain, by cutting flesh and passing between the pieces)."[7] In other words 'karath' means to make a covenant by sacrifice.

Now, we know from Scripture that after the coming of the Messiah, He laid down His life as an offering for the forgiveness of sin.

> "Just as Christ loved us and gave himself up for us as a fragrant offering and sacrifice to God." (Ephesians 5:2)

---

[7] Strong's Concordance transliterated Hebrew and Greek - *karath*: H3772

So what is the connection between the Hebrew word 'karath' and the sacrifice which Christ made for sin? The meaning of 'karath' is a perfect description of what the Messiah did when He went to the cross. Since 'karath' means to make a covenant by sacrifice we can understand Daniel 9:26 to say, after 483 years, Messiah the King will make a covenant by sacrifice and will have nothing. This is exactly what happened after He entered Jerusalem on April 6, 32 AD. He then made a covenant in His own blood on the cross for the forgiveness of sin. This covenant, for the forgiveness of sin, is still available today for all who would receive it by faith.

Destruction of Jerusalem and the Temple

Next Daniel tells us that after the Messiah makes a covenant by sacrifice, the people of the ruler who will come will destroy Jerusalem and the temple.

> "The people of the ruler who will come will destroy the city and the sanctuary. The end will come like a flood: War will continue until the end, and desolations have been decreed." (Daniel 9:26)

Jesus also predicted the same destruction of Jerusalem and the temple, when He told the chief priests and the teachers of the law that this destruction would be the result of their failing to know and understand this prophecy. Remember, God had told them in Daniel "**To know and understand**." And they did not!

"The days will come upon you when your enemies will build an embankment against you and encircle you and hem you in on every side. They will dash you to the ground, you and the children within your walls. They will not leave one stone on another, **because you did not recognize the time of God's coming to you.**" (Luke 19:43, 44)

In 70 AD, just as Jesus and Daniel predicted, the Roman army under General Titus came to besiege Jerusalem.[8] The Jewish historian, Flavius Josephus, documented this event, estimating that 1,100,000 Jews were killed in the destruction of Jerusalem and the temple.[9] He recorded that the Syrians in the Roman army set fire to the temple causing the gold in the temple to melt down into the cracks of the stonework. The Roman army then took down every stone one from another to get the gold, just as Jesus had predicted, see Luke 19:44 above.

After Daniel predicts the destruction of Jerusalem and the temple in verse twenty-six, he says "the end will come like a flood: War will continue until the end, and desolations have been decreed."

This description sounds much like what Christ said would mark the Time of the End, from its beginning to the End. Christ said,

---

[8] Flavius Josephus, The complete Works, Book 5

[9] Flavius, Book 6.9.3

"Nation will rise against nation [revolutions], and kingdom against kingdom [wars]. There will be famines and earthquakes in various places. All these are the beginning of birth pains." (Matthew 24:6)

Interruption in Daniel's 70 'sevens'

So, at this point 483 years of the 490-year prophecy have been fulfilled. Now, if the last seven years of the 490-year prophecy had run continuously they would have been completed from 32 AD to 39 AD. However, thirty-eight more years elapsed before the destruction of Jerusalem and the Temple in 70 AD and the final seven years of the prophecy remained unfulfilled.

The timeline below depicts Daniel's Seventy Sevens prophecy with the interruption between the first sixty-nine "*sevens*" and the 70th "*seven*".

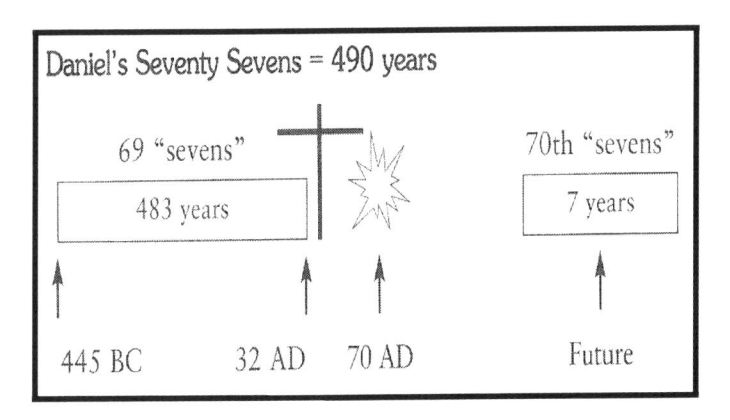

```
Daniel's Seventy Sevens = 490 years

    69 "sevens"                        70th "sevens"
    ┌─────────────┐                    ┌─────────────┐
    │  483 years  │                    │   7 years   │
    └─────────────┘                    └─────────────┘
       ↑           ↑     ↑                   ↑
    445 BC      32 AD  70 AD              Future
```

Note: The reason 445 BC plus 32 AD doesn't equal 483 years is due to difference between the biblical (lunar) and modern (solar) calendar.

The interruption in this prophecy is not unique to Scripture. As a matter of fact, the interruption between the two Advents of the Messiah is actually found several times in Scripture. One example comes from John the Baptist when he described two aspects of the ministry of the Messiah.

> "He will baptize you with the Holy Spirit **[interruption]** and with fire. His winnowing fork is in his hand, and he will clear his threshing floor, gathering his wheat into the barn and burning up the chaff with unquenchable fire." (Matthew 3:11-12)

This prophecy from John the Baptist reveals that the Messiah will first baptize us with the Holy Spirit, which He fulfilled on the day of Pentecost almost 2,000 years ago. The second part of this prophecy states that He will baptize us with fire, which He will do on the Day of the Lord when the Messiah will judge His people by fire. See how Paul describes this below.

> "Every man's work shall be made manifest: for the day shall declare it, because it shall be revealed by fire; and the fire shall try every man's work of what sort it is. If any man's work abide which he hath built thereupon, he shall receive a reward. If any man's work shall be burned, he shall suffer loss: but he himself shall be saved; yet so as by fire." (1 Corinthians 3:13-15)

Another example is found in the Gospel of Luke. Jesus revealed that He was fulfilling Scripture in the people's hearing when He read from the prophecies of Isaiah. He did not, however, finish reading the complete prophecy as recorded in Isaiah 61. He stopped in mid sentence at the point where it says "Yahweh's favor."

The reason He did not continue reading the remainder of Isaiah's prophecy is because the remainder of the prophecy would not be fulfilled until His return on the Day of the Lord. Compare the passage in Luke's record with Isaiah's prophecy and see the interruption between the first and second advents.

> 'The Spirit of the Lord is on me, because he has anointed me to preach good news to the poor. He has sent me to proclaim freedom for the prisoners and recovery of sight for the blind, to release the oppressed, to proclaim the year of Yahweh's favor.' **[interruption]** Then he rolled up the scroll gave it back to the attendant and sat down. The eyes of everyone in the synagogue were fastened on him, and he began by saying to them, 'Today this scripture is fulfilled in your hearing.'" (Luke 4:18-21)

> "To proclaim the year of Yahweh's favor **[interruption]** and the day of vengeance of our God, to comfort all who mourn, and provide for those who grieve in Zion." (Isaiah 61:2, 3)

The Messiah fulfilled the first part of Isaiah's prophecy "the year of Yahweh's favor" at His First Coming. The second part, "the day of vengeance," He will fulfill at His Second Coming on the Day of the Lord.

As we can see these prophecies have two parts with an interruption separating the two Advents of Christ. The first part of each was fulfilled about 2,000 years ago in relationship to Christ's First Coming and the second part will be fulfilled at the Christ's Second Coming on the Day of Yahweh (the LORD).

We are currently living in the interruption between the two advents of the Messiah. We also know that several prophesied events have already occurred during this interruption period. The first was when the Messiah made the New Covenant in His blood on the cross. The next was the destruction of Jerusalem and the temple in 70 AD.

Recently, Israel's restoration to their land as a nation on May 14, 1948 is most likely a fulfillment of these biblical prophecies:

> "The days are coming, declares Yahweh, when I will bring my people Israel and Judah back from captivity and restore them to the land I gave their forefathers to possess, says Yahweh" (Jeremiah 30:3)

> "Therefore say: 'This is what the Sovereign Yahweh says: I will gather you from the nations and bring you back from the countries where you have been scattered, and I will give you back the land of Israel again.'" (Ezekiel 11:17)

This brings us to Daniel's 70th 'seven', a key to understanding the last seven years which lead to the return of the Messiah.

Now, let's do a quick review of Daniel's 70 'sevens' before we examine the last 'seven', Daniel's 70th 'seven."

Daniel's 70 'sevens' Prophecy

In this prophecy Yahweh, the God of the Bible, indicated exactly when the Messiah's First Coming would occur, and He provided key signs to the Messiah's Second Coming.

The prophecy opens with a statement of its duration, broken into seventy 'sevens' of years. Then it speaks of God's ultimate promise for His People and the Holy city of Jerusalem.

> "Seventy 'sevens' are decreed for your people and your holy city to finish transgression, to put an end to sin, to atone for wickedness, to bring in everlasting righteousness, to seal up vision and prophecy and to anoint the most holy." (Daniel 9:24)

In the first verse, Daniel is told that 70 'sevens' must be fulfilled and then God will restore everything that He has promised to Israel and the people of God.

Daniel was told that from the decree to rebuild Jerusalem, which is recorded in Nehemiah 2:5-8, to the Messiah's coming would be 483 years. This part of the prophecy was fulfilled in 32 A.D., exactly as indicated. Then Daniel was told:

> "After the sixty-two 'sevens,' the Anointed One will be cut off [make a covenant] and will have nothing." (Daniel 9:26)

After the Messiah came in 32 A.D., He made a covenant by sacrifice, His death on the cross. Then we are told that:

> The people, of **the ruler who will come** [Antichrist], will destroy the city and the sanctuary." (Daniel 9:26)

Just as prophesied, Jerusalem and the Jewish Temple were destroyed in 70 A.D. by the Syrian troops in the Roman Army under General Titus.

According to the historian Josephus, in 70 A.D. the Syrians who were conscripts in the Roman Army of General Titus are the people who destroyed Jerusalem and the Jewish Temple, exactly as prophesied.

Antichrist and the Last Seven Years

This prophecy also connects "the people" (the ancient Syrians), with "the ruler who will come" (the Antichrist). We know that this coming ruler will be the future Antichrist because his actions are described in the next verse of the prophecy.

Now, let's look at the last seven years.

Daniel's 70th 'seven' Prophecy

In Daniel 9:27 we are told about the last seven years of the prophecy. The last 7 years of Daniel's prophecy did not follow directly after the previous 483 years. As a matter of fact, the last 7 years have never been fulfilled and they remain to be fulfilled in the future. When the last seven years are fulfilled, God's promise to Jerusalem and His people will be complete.

Below is what Daniel was told about the final 7 years. Once again, the "he" in this passage is the Antichrist, "the ruler who will come" from verse 9:26.

> "**He** (Antichrist) will confirm a covenant with many for one 'seven.' In the middle of the 'seven' **he** will put an end to sacrifice and offering. And on a wing of the temple **he** will set up an abomination that causes desolation, until the end that is decreed is poured out on **him**." (Daniel 9:27)

```
┌─────────────────────────────────────────────────────────┐
│ Daniel's 70 'seven Timeline                             │
│                                                         │
│                                        End of the Age   │
│                  Daniel's 70th 'seven'                  │
│  ──────────────────────────────────────────────────►    │
│         │ 3 1/2 yrs of Peace │ Great Tribulation │      │
│                                                         │
│         ▲              ▲                  ▲             │
│         │              │                  │             │
│      Covenant     Abomination that     The end         │
│      Confirmed    causes desolation                    │
└─────────────────────────────────────────────────────────┘
```

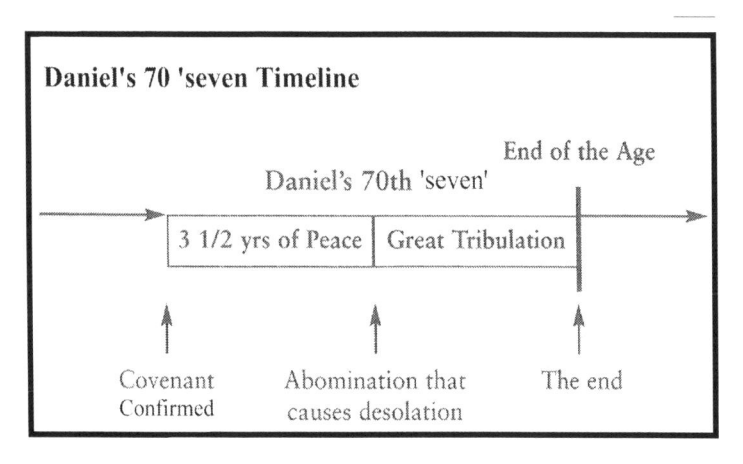

In the very near future this ruler (Antichrist) will arise as a descendent of the people of ancient Syria. Then He will confirm an existing treaty for Israel's safety. After 3.5 years he will stop temple worship and set himself up in the Jewish Temple proclaiming that he is God. This event is called the abomination that causes desolation. The Antichrist will be successful at everything he does until the End, when the Messiah will return and pour out His wrath on him.

As we know Daniel's seventy sevens prophecy foretold the precise timing of the Messiah's First Coming. It also provides the timing to His Second Coming when the Messiah will come, defeat the Antichrist and his armies and pour out His wrath on the disobedient and unbelieving world.

What we know about the 70 'sevens':

- 70 'sevens' is 70 'sevens' of years or 490 years.
- 483 of the 490 years have been fulfilled.

- 7 years of this prophecy remain unfulfilled.
- The 7 years starts when the Antichrist confirms an existing covenant.
- In the middle of the 7 Antichrist will set up the 'abomination that causes desolation.'

Chapter 7

Antichrist's Last 3.5 Years

"Daniel, the words are closed up and sealed
  until the time of the end."
                                Daniel 12:9

The final prophecy of Daniel opens with a description of the Great Tribulation. It begins with Michael the Archangel arising to take action and closes with all Yahweh's people being resurrected to eternal life. Let's read the first two verses.

> "At that time Michael, the great prince who protects your people, will arise. **There will be a time of tribulation such as has not happened from the beginning** of nations until then. But at that time your people--everyone whose name is found written in the book--will be delivered. Multitudes who sleep in the dust of the earth will awake: some to everlasting life, others to shame and everlasting contempt." (Daniel 12:1-2)

The first thing I should point out is that Christ used almost the same words when He named the Great Tribulation in the Gospel of Matthew. Here is what He said,

> "For then **there will be great tribulation, unequaled from the beginning** of the world until now--and never to be equaled again." (Matthew 24:21)

The first part of Daniel's prophecy places Michael the Archangel at the beginning of the Great Tribulation. This corresponds perfectly with a prophecy about Michael in Revelation 12. In Revelation we are given more details about what happens when Michael is called to action, as we see here.

> "And there was war in heaven. **Michael and his angels fought against the dragon,** and the dragon and his angels fought back. But he was not strong enough, and they lost their place in heaven. **The great dragon was hurled down**--that ancient serpent called the devil, or Satan, who leads the whole world astray. He was hurled to the earth, and his angels with him." (Revelation 12:7-9)

Michael and his angels throw Satan and his angels from heaven to earth. When Satan is thrown out of heaven to earth, the Great Tribulation begins and the situation will become very bad for Yahweh's people. The apostle Paul also described this situation when the Antichrist would be revealed, as we read below:

> **"The coming of the lawless one (Antichrist) will be in accordance with the work of Satan** displayed in all kinds of counterfeit miracles, signs and wonders, and in every sort of evil that deceives those who are perishing." (2 Thessalonians 2:9-10)

The Revelation prophecy describes when Michael throws Satan from heaven to earth. The timing of this event is yet another prophecy which identifies that the Great Tribulation will be 3.5 years in duration, as we see below:

> "When the dragon (Satan) saw that he had been hurled to the earth, he pursued the woman (Israel) who had given birth to the male child. The woman was given the two wings of a great eagle, so that she might fly to the place prepared for her in the desert, where she would be taken care of **for a time, times and half a time** (3.5 years), out of the serpent's reach." (Revelation 12:13-14)

The Revelation prophecy concerning Michael and Satan even uses the same **time, times and half a time** reference for 3.5 years that we saw in Daniel 12:7.

The next verse in Daniel addresses leading many to righteousness. For a comprehensive commentary on End Time biblical righteousness read the "<u>Watchman's Guide to End Time Repentance</u>."

> "Those who are wise will shine like the brightness of the heavens, and those who lead many to righteousness, like the stars for ever and ever." (Daniel 12:3)

Below Daniel is told when Yahweh's prophetic words will be unsealed and opened. He is also told something that many teachers today do not understand because they get their understanding from other men, not the Word of Yahweh. Let's take a look at the prophecy and I will show you what I mean.

> "But you, Daniel, close up and seal the words of the scroll until the time of the end. **Many will go here and there to increase knowledge.**" (Daniel 12:3-4)

I cannot tell you how many times I have heard, over the years, teachers and pastors saying something like this:

> *"God is telling Daniel how it will be in the Last Days. Knowledge will increase. As we see today with television, the internet, cell phones and technological breakthroughs in the sciences. People are going here and there, travel is faster and more frequent. Clearly this is an indication that we are in the Last Days."*

This mistaken idea has come from Man. It is not what this prophecy is saying. The prophecy was written in Hebrew. This is a Hebrew expression which describes someone searching for knowledge from Scripture, going back and forth across the lines to gain understanding. When we understand its meaning we will see that it fits perfectly in context with the rest of the prophecy. It also tells Yahweh's people what they must do at the Time of the End; read and understand Scripture.

Now, let's get to the question that is raised in the prophecy.

> "How long will it be before these astonishing things are fulfilled?" (Daniel 12:6)

The answer came that explained how long the Great Tribulation will last from the time that it starts.

> **"It will be for a time, times and half a time** (3.5 years). When the power of the holy people has been finally broken, all these things will be completed." (Daniel 12:7)

From this prophecy we have seen that it starts when Michael arises and from other prophecies it starts with the "abomination that causes desolation."

Below Daniel was told again when the words would be opened and unsealed. He was also told that only those who were truly Yahweh's people will understand.

> "Go your way, Daniel, because **the words are closed up and sealed until the time of the end**. Many will be purified, made spotless and refined, but the wicked will continue to be wicked. None of the wicked will understand, but those who are wise will understand." (Daniel 12:9-10)

The next part of the prophecy is very interesting because it indicates that there will be some time between the end of the 3.5 years of the Great Tribulation and the Day of the LORD, when Yahweh's people will be blessed.

First, let me say that I do not fully understand the significance of the 1,290 days and the 1,335 days.

However, I will share with you what I currently understand about this prophecy. The Antichrist causes sacrifice in the temple to cease in the middle of the last seven years when he sets up the "abomination that causes desolation." The 3.5 years of the Great Tribulation is 1,260 days as we are told in Revelation below:

> "But exclude the outer court; do not measure it, because it has been given to the Gentiles. They will trample on the holy city for 42 months (3.5 years). And I will give power to my two witnesses, and they will prophesy for **1,260 days** (3.5 years), clothed in sackcloth." (Revelation 11:2-3)

> "The woman (Israel) fled into the desert to a place prepared for her by God, where she might be taken care of for **1,260 days** (3.5 years)." (Revelation 12:6)

With the 1,260 days in mind, let read the prophecy.

> **"From the time that the daily sacrifice is abolished and the abomination that causes desolation is set up**, there will be **1,290 days**. Blessed is the one who waits for and reaches the **end of the 1,335 days**. As for you, go your way till the end. You will rest, and then at the end of the days you will rise to receive your allotted inheritance." (Daniel 12:11-13)

While, everything in this prophecy is not yet clear, it is clear that there will be 75 days (1,335 – 1,260 = 75) between the end of the Great Tribulation and the Day of the LORD, when Yahweh's people will be blessed. It is my understanding that Yahweh's people will be blessed when the Messiah returns and delivers them into His kingdom. Therefore, there will be 75 days between the end of the Great Tribulation and the Second Coming.

This idea has good Scriptural support. If we compare Scripture with Scripture we see that there will be time between the end of the Great Tribulation and the Messiah's return. Let me show you.

First, here is what the Messiah, called Christ, said would happen immediately after the Great Tribulation:

> "**Immediately <u>after</u> the tribulation** of those days '"the <u>sun will be darkened, and the moon will not give its light; the stars will fall from the sky</u>, and the heavenly bodies will be shaken." (Matthew 24:29)

This is a specific sign that has been spoken of by the prophets which will come before the "Day of Yahweh" better known as the "Day of the LORD." For example, the prophet Joel wrote this about the sign in the sun, moon and stars with regard to the "Day of Yahweh."

> **"The sun will be turned to darkness and the moon to blood <u>before</u> the coming of the great and dreadful day of Yahweh (Day of the LORD).** And everyone who calls on the name of Yahweh will be saved; for on Mount Zion and in Jerusalem there will be deliverance." (Joel 2:31-32)

I am showing you a couple of passages which seem to correspond to Daniel 12, to illustrate the point that there will be some time after the Great Tribulation but before the Second Coming.

What we now know:

- Michael takes action and the Great Tribulation begins.

- There will be 75 days between the Great Tribulation and the Second Coming.

- Only Yahweh's people will know the truth.

- The words are closed and sealed until the Time of the End.

Daniel's Timeline

We have carefully examined each of Daniel's prophecies concerning the Antichrist. Now, I would like to visually present several of Daniel's future prophecies in chronological order. I'll call this Daniel's End Time Timeline.

Daniel was **not** told when the Time of the End would begin, however he was given several prophecies about the beast known as the Antichrist leading up to the end and the coming Kingdom of God on earth.

Let's look at the timeline and then I will list the major prophetic events in chronological order; starting with the fourth beast kingdom of the Antichrist through to the end and the Second Coming.

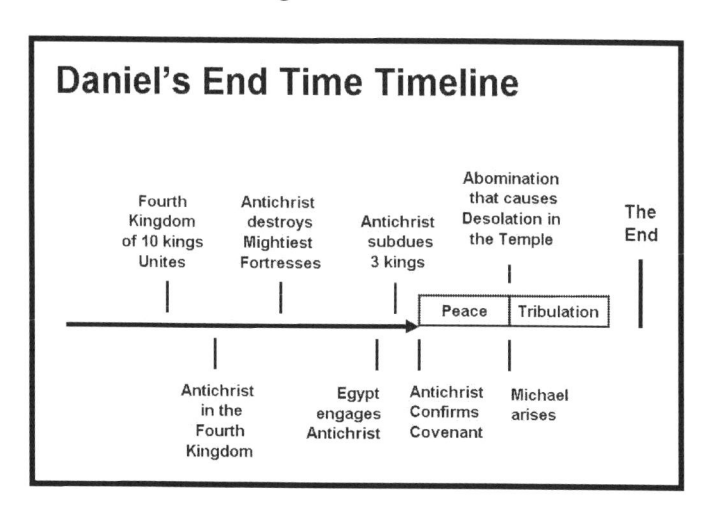

Daniel's End Time Timeline

Above timeline (left to right): Fourth Kingdom of 10 kings Unites | Antichrist destroys Mightiest Fortresses | Antichrist subdues 3 kings | Abomination that causes Desolation in the Temple | The End

Below timeline (left to right): Antichrist in the Fourth Kingdom | Egypt engages Antichrist | Antichrist Confirms Covenant | Michael arises

Between Covenant and The End: Peace | Tribulation

- Fourth Kingdom of Antichrist with 10 kings.

- Antichrist arises among the 10 Kings.

- Antichrist Destroys the Mightiest Fortresses.

- King of Egypt engages the Antichrist.

- Antichrist subdues the 3 kings: Egypt, Libya and Sudan.

- Antichrist invades Israel and Confirms a Covenant.

- Michael arises and Antichrist sets up "abomination that causes desolation.

- The End: Messiah returns and establishes Yahweh's eternal Kingdom on earth.

At the end of all Daniel's prophecies, Yahweh left Daniel with this final message:

> "Go your way, Daniel, because the words are closed up and sealed until the time of the end."
> Daniel 12:9

In the next chapter I will show from Scripture what Yahweh has revealed to me about the Seals of Revelation and what we need to learn from them.

This revelation concerning Revelation's first four seals is new and has only recently been revealed by Yahweh. I am including this revelation about the seals because the first four seal provide an important Time of the End timeline concerning the Antichrist which will prove critical to Yahweh's people.

Chapter 8

Seal Wars before Antichrist

"Daniel, the words are closed up and sealed until the time of the end."   Daniel 12:9

The Time of the End Has Come!

In this chapter we will be examining Revelation's seven seals. The Seven Seals span the Time of the End. We will see as we examine the seal prophecies that the First Seal marks the beginning of the Time of the End and the Seventh Seal the end.

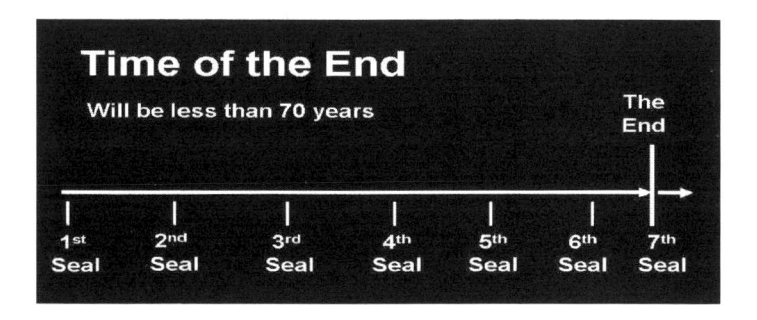

Time of the End
Will be less than 70 years — The End

1st Seal | 2nd Seal | 3rd Seal | 4th Seal | 5th Seal | 6th Seal | 7th Seal

Before we discuss the First Seal, let me show you what the Lord taught me about the horses and riders of Revelation's first four seal prophecies. Since this is a new teaching on Revelation, I will show you from Scripture how I was led to this understanding.

Horses and Riders

As we read the first four seal prophecies, we notice that all four have some things in common. As each seal is opened a different colored horse comes forth. The first horse is white, the second fiery red, the third black and the fourth pale. We are also told that each horse has a rider.

Therefore, if we hope to understand the meaning of these first four seal prophecies we must know the answer to these two questions:

- **What do the four colored horses symbolize?**

- **What does a horse and rider symbolize?**

First, what is symbolized by the colored horses? Do they tell us something we need to know in order to understand these prophecies?

The four colored horses symbolize something very important to a correct understanding of the first four seal prophecies. To understand what the four colored horses symbolize, let's search Scripture to see if God tells us about these four colored horses. Is there any other place in Scripture that mentions four colored horses?

There is only one other place in Scripture which makes reference to four different colored horses. We find them described in Zechariah's prophecies. Zechariah received many prophecies from Yahweh about the Time of the End, many of which correspond to prophecies recorded in the book of Revelation.

In our particular example, Zechariah saw four colored horses. The horses in Zechariah's vision appear to be similar or even the same as the four colored horses in Revelation. Zechariah was told several things about the four different colored horses. Here is what he wrote:

> "I looked up again--and there before me were four chariots coming out from between two mountains--mountains of bronze! The first chariot had red horses, the second black, the third white, and the fourth dappled--all of them powerful. I asked the angel who was speaking to me, 'What are these, my lord?' The angel answered me, **'These are the four spirits of heaven, going out from standing in the presence of the Lord of the whole world**. The one with the black horses is going toward the north country, the one with the white horses toward the west, and the one with the dappled horses toward the south." (Zechariah 6:1-8)

The four colored horses; red, black, white and dappled **are the four spirits** of heaven that go out to the whole world, north, south, east and west. The black horses go to the north, the white go toward the west and the dappled to the south which leaves the red horses to go toward the east.

Some Bible translations state that the white horses go toward the west and some do not. Because, there is no other place in Scripture that provides a direct connection to the four colored horses of Revelation, we should take this information into consideration as we attempt to understand the significance of the horses of Revelation.

There is also a slight difference in the prophet's descriptions of one of the four horses. In Revelation John describes one of the horses as pale. In Zechariah the prophet describes this horse as dappled. Could these two seemingly different descriptions of Revelation's fourth horse actually be of the same horse? Only God knows. However, since this is the only other place where Yahweh tells us about four colored horses, we should keep it in mind as we examine the first four seals of Revelation.

Where were the horses assigned?

According to Zechariah 6, the horses **are the four spirits** of heaven that go out from the Lord. The white horses go to the west, the red horses go to the east, the black horses go to the north and the dappled go to the south.

Assigned to the West, East, North and South of where?

Unless otherwise stated, biblical prophecies are written from the perspective of Jerusalem, Israel. This means that the four colored horses have been assigned to the west, east, north and south of Israel as geographically displayed on the map below:

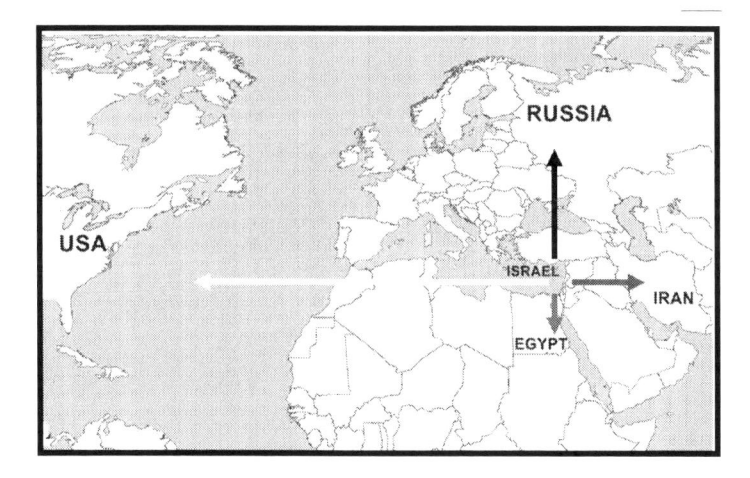

Now, we know where in the world the four colored horses were assigned by God. With this information we can know where to look as Christ opens each of the first four seals.

1. When the first seal opens, look to the West
2. When the second seal opens, look to the East.
3. When the third seal opens, look to the North.
4. When the fourth seal opens, look to the South.

Just as each of the first seals of Revelation has a horse, each horse has a rider. To understand these prophecies, we need to know the symbolism of "horse and rider."

What's a horse and rider?

Once again we are very fortunate because Yahweh has used the term "horse and rider" to describe both historical as well as prophetic events. Here is an historical example from Exodus:

> "Then Moses and the Israelites sang this song to Yahweh: I will sing to Yahweh, for he is highly exalted. **The horse and its rider** he has hurled into the sea. … **Pharaoh**'s chariots **and his army** he has hurled into the sea." (Exodus 15:1-4)

In the Exodus story, Pharaoh is the rider and his army is the horse.

These next two examples are prophecies which further illustrate how God uses "horse and rider" to symbolize nation's armies and their leaders.

> "You are my war club, my weapon for battle-- with you I shatter nations, with you I destroy kingdoms, with you **I shatter horse and rider**, with you I shatter chariot and driver." (Jeremiah 51:20-21)

> "On that day I will strike **every horse with panic and its rider with madness**," declares Yahweh. "I will keep a watchful eye over the house of Judah, but I will blind all the horses of the nations." (Zechariah 12:4)

These descriptions of "horse and rider" in prophecy clearly indicate that God uses "horse and rider" to represent a nation's army and its leader.

Therefore, as we examine the horses and riders of Revelation's first four seals we can now understand what they symbolize.

- Horse = A nation's Military
- Rider = A nation's Leader

As each seal is opened, a national leader and his army will begin to fulfill the prophecy described in Revelation chapter six. Therefore, as each seal is opened another leader and his army will start another war in the Time of the End.

First Seal Prophecy

Here is how the first seal prophecy is described in Revelation:

> "I watched as the Lamb opened the first of the seven seals. Then I heard one of the four living creatures say in a voice like thunder, 'Come!' I looked, and there before me was a white horse! Its rider held a bow, and he was given a crown, and he rode out as a conqueror bent on conquest." (Revelation 6:1-2)

Rider on the White Horse

When Christ opened the first of the seven seals, we are told that the white horse has a rider. The rider on the white horse was a leader from the West of Israel.

What Man Thinks

Before we continue, let's look at a common mistake that has been made when trying to identify the rider on the white horse. This error in interpretation was made hundreds of years ago. Unfortunately, it is still being repeated today by many teachers who rely on the teachings of man over the Word of God.

In the book of Revelation we find that there are two riders on white horses. The first rider is one we have seen in Revelation's First Seal prophecy. The second rider is found in Revelation chapter nineteen. Below is the description of the second horse and rider:

> "I saw heaven standing open and there before me was a white horse, whose **rider is called Faithful and True**. With justice he judges and makes war. His eyes are like blazing fire, and on his head are many crowns. He has a name written on him that no one knows but he himself. He is dressed in a robe dipped in blood, and **his name is the Word of God.**" (Revelation 19:11-13)

This second rider is Christ, the Word of God.

Because the second rider is clearly Christ, some people have assumed that the first rider on the white horse must also be Christ. However, many people today have been told that the first rider is not Christ and therefore, he must be a false Christ. That is why so many people think the first rider on the white horse is Antichrist.

These people appear to be using Scripture to make their interpretation. However, they are taking the prophecy out of context and jumping to conclusions without carefully examining what Scripture says. The first seal prophecy is not just about a white horse and its rider. In its context the prophecy is about four colored horses and their riders. Therefore, **we must look at all four horses** and riders to understand what Yahweh is saying, not just one horse and rider, but all four.

Mistaking the first horse and rider for Christ or the Antichrist leads people into very serious mistakes.

Many who interpret this first rider as Christ tend to believe the prophecy started about 2,000 years ago with Christ. These people are called "Preterists" because they see Revelation's prophecies as being about the past, thinking that they were written about Rome's persecution of the Church.

Others who believe that the first rider on the white horse is the Antichrist, assume that the seven seals only span the last seven years when the Antichrist appears and rules the whole world. These people are called "Dispensationalists" or "Pre-Tribulationists" because they believe that the "Rapture" of the Church will occur before the last seven years when the Antichrist will be in power.

However, both of these old teachings of man are inconsistent with what Yahweh says in Scripture.

What God Says

As we will see from Scripture, the seals will span a much longer period of time than just the last seven years. The seals will span the entire Time of the End which Christ said would last less than a generation. Therefore, as we will see, the First Seal started the Time of the End and the Seventh Seal will close the Time of the End.

Based on this new interpretation from Scripture, the white horse and rider represents an army and its leader from the West.

He was holding a Bow

We are also told in the first seal prophecy (Revelation 6:1-2) that the "rider held a bow." It appears that this bow could have two symbolic meanings.

First, a bow is a military weapon and has military symbolism. However, in our prophecy, this military symbolism is redundant in the prophecy because we already know that the riders of the horses are leaders of armies. Since we already know that, it is more likely that God is telling us something else that will help us.

The second symbolic meaning seems to indicate that this bow is God's bow and when Yahweh uncovers His bow the Time of the End will begin. This means that the bow has spiritual significance in a similar way as the four colored horses of Zechariah 6.

Below is an End Time prophecy from Habakkuk that gives the impression that the bow is spiritual and it belongs to Yahweh. See what you think:

> "Were you angry with the rivers, O Yahweh? Was your wrath against the streams? Did you rage against the sea when you rode with your horses and your victorious chariots? **You uncovered your bow**, you called for many arrows." (Habakkuk 3:8-9)

Therefore, when the first seal was opened, the rider on the white horse was the commander-in-chief of the military from the west and had something to do with **Yahweh uncovering His bow**. I interpret this as symbolizing the start of the Time of the End. If so, the First Seal was the first prophecy of the Time of the End.

What happened after the first seal was opened?

He was given a Crown

Then the rider on the white horse was "given a crown." The Greek word for crown in this verse indicates that it is a victor's crown.

Which means that sometime after the first seal was opened the leader from the west won a victory, "he was given a crown".

What else happened?

He Rode Out as a Conqueror

After the first seal was opened, the leader from the west "rode out as a conqueror." He left his country in the west and went out to another country as a conqueror. But that's not all.

He was Bent on Conquest

Not only did he go out as a conqueror, but we he was also "bent on conquest." In other words, he was determined to conquer in war.

Now that we have reviewed each detail of the first Seal Prophecy from Revelation, let's see how this prophecy was fulfilled.

First Seal Prophecy Fulfilled

The white horse was assigned to the west of Israel. Due west from Israel, as we can see from the map below, is the United States of America.

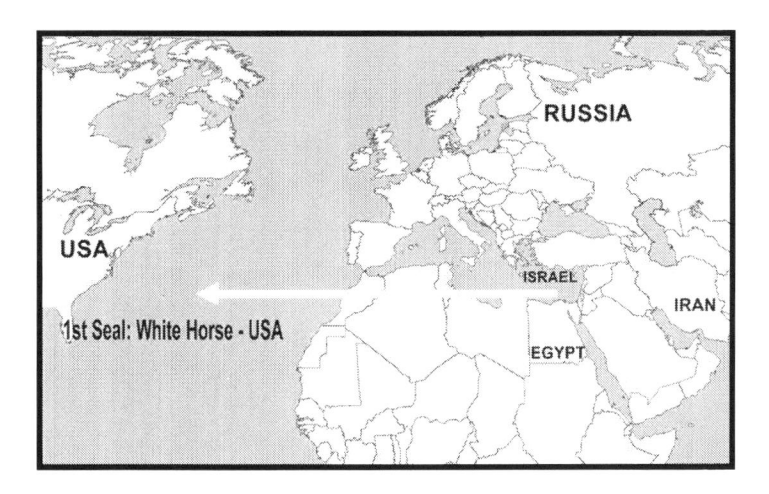

The events of this prophecy relate to the United States of America and its leader at the time the First Seal was opened.

When was the first seal opened?

Rider in the White House

On September 11, 2001, Christ opened the first seal of Revelation. When He opened the first seal the rider on the white horse was holding a bow. On 9/11/2001 the President of the United States was the Commander-in-Chief of the U.S. Military and he was about to start a war that would begin End Time events.

After the First Seal was opened on 9/11, "he was given a crown." In 2004, George W. Bush won an election and a second term as President of the United States and Commander-in-Chief of the U.S. Military. After 9/11 he received a victor's crown.

What else happen after 9/11?

Rode out as a Conqueror

After the first seal opened on 9/11, the Commander-in-Chief "rode out as a conqueror." In 2001, under his leadership, the U.S. Military went to Afghanistan and drove Al Qaeda out of that country.

Then again, after 9/11, the Commander-in-Chief "rode out as a conqueror." In 2003 the U.S. Military attacked and conquered Iraq and Saddam Hussein, the President of Iraq.

Determined to Win the War on Terror

Also, during his two terms as President and Commander-in-Chief of the U.S. Military, the rider on the white horse, remained "bent on conquest." He was determined to win the "War on Terror" which he had declared.

These recent historical events precisely fulfilled each detail of the first seal prophecy of the Book of Revelation. Let's review the prophecy one more time so we have this clearly in mind:

> "I looked, and there before me was a white horse! Its rider held a bow, and he was given a crown, and he rode out as a conqueror bent on conquest." (Revelation 6:2)

The first seal of Revelation is the first of three major prophecies which identify and confirm that the Time of the End has indeed come.

There are other prophecies which also point to the 9/11 event, when the first seal of Revelation was opened. This prophecy below appears to reference the collapse of the Twin Towers in New York City on 9/11. Here is how the prophecy reads:

> "Take up your positions around **Babylon**, all you who draw the bow. Shoot at her! Spare no arrows, for she has sinned against Yahweh. Shout against her on every side! ... **her towers fall.**" (Jeremiah 50:14-15)

Another aspect of Zechariah's prophecy could also point to the twin towers. This may add further support to this interpretation.

Let's take a close look at Zechariah 6 again.

"I looked up again--and there before me were four chariots **coming out from between two mountains-- mountains of bronze**! The first chariot had red horses, the second black, the third white, and the fourth dappled--all of them powerful. I asked the angel who was speaking to me, 'What are these, my lord?' The angel answered me, 'These are the four spirits of heaven, going out from standing in the presence of the Lord of the whole world. The one with the black horses is going toward the north country, the one with the white horses toward the west, and the one with the dappled horses toward the south" (Zechariah 6:1-8).

If we note that "bronze" is a man-made metal, then we could understand this verse to say something like this,

"I looked up again--and there before me were four chariots **coming out from between two man made mountains."** Or.

I looked up again--and there before me were four chariots coming out from between the twin towers of the World Trade Center.

From what we read in Scripture and the historical events since 9/11, the fulfillment of the first seal prophecy appears to serve as the first prophetic witness to the Time of the End.

Below is how this appears on a timeline.

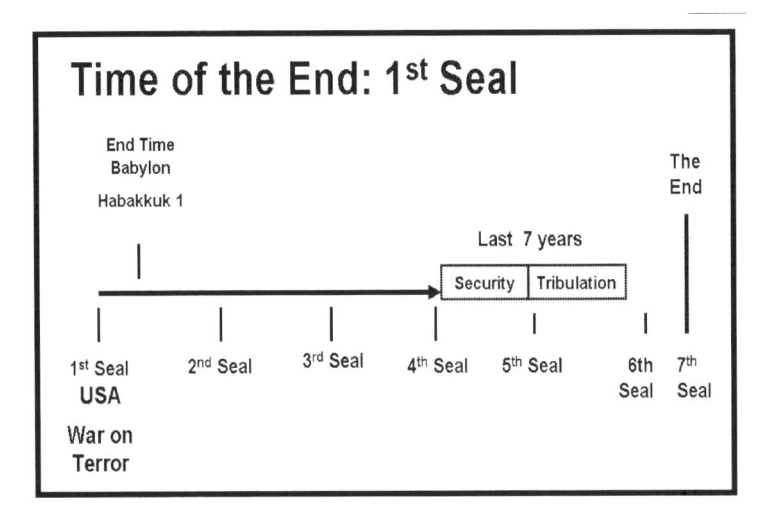

```
Time of the End: 1st Seal

End Time
Babylon                                                    The
Habakkuk 1                                                 End
                                        Last 7 years
                                      Security | Tribulation
 |           |          |          |          |        |    |
1st Seal   2nd Seal   3rd Seal   4th Seal   5th Seal  6th  7th
 USA                                                  Seal  Seal
War on
Terror
```

Before we examine the Second Seal which is the next Time of the End prophecy to be fulfilled, I would like to point out something else we should know about the First Seal prophecy. The prophet Habakkuk also wrote about events that would take place after the First Seal was opened. Compare Habakkuk's first chapter to what happened when the U.S. Military went out conquering following 9/11.

Don't forget Habakkuk.

Here is some of what Habakkuk wrote about that.

> "**I am raising up the Babylonians**, that ruthless and impetuous people, **who sweep across the whole earth** to seize dwelling places not their own. They are a feared and dreaded people; **they are a law to themselves** and promote their own honor. Their horses are swifter than leopards, fiercer than wolves at dusk. Their cavalry gallops headlong; **their horsemen come from afar**. **They fly like a vulture swooping to devour**; they all come bent on violence. **Their hordes advance like a desert wind** and gather prisoners like sand. They deride kings and scoff at rulers. They laugh at all fortified cities; they build earthen ramps and capture them. Then they sweep past like the wind and go on-- guilty men, whose own strength is their god." (Habakkuk 1:6-11)

I should point out that Habakkuk's prophecies are specifically stated by God to be about the Babylonians (Habakkuk 1:6) and about the appointed Time of the End (Habakkuk 2:3).

Before we move on, let me share with you something I saw that I believe offers even more support to the idea that 9/11 marked the opening of the First Seal.

It's a Youtube.com video titled, "ASTOUNDING REVELATION - GOD'S JUDGMENT ON AMERICA – REVEALED"[3]

Missed Wake Up Call.

---

[3] http://www.youtube.com/watch?v=JW6roFN7NAE&list=FLXNJGzvnMfDY9yUUmjLvQWA&index=1&feature=plpp_video

The First Seal prophecy was God's first wake up call for His people. If the Church had been awake as Christ commanded, they could have recognized that the First Seal Prophecy had been fulfilled. However, the Church was not awake and they failed to recognize from Scripture what had happened.

Not only was the Church asleep but they also failed to wake up. When the First Seal opened on 9/11 many of the churches initially appeared to be waking up as they began to seek God in prayer. This continued for several months. It was as though the churches were trying to awaken. However, they did not wake up and within a year following 9/11 all the churches had returned to their deep sleep, doing just what they had been doing before the First Seal opened.

Christ wanted His Church to be awake. When Christ was telling His followers about the Time of the End, He warned them to stay awake, be alert and keep watch.

Mark's gospel captures Christ's warning,

> "**Be on guard! Be alert**! **You do not know when that time will come**. … Therefore **keep watch** because you do not know when the owner of the house will come back … If he comes suddenly, **do not let him find you sleeping.** What I say to you, I say to everyone: **'Watch!'**" (Mark 13:33-37)

Christ wanted His Church to be awake. But, He also knew that they would **not** be awake when the Time of the End began. Therefore, He planned to wake them when He opened Revelation's Second Seal.

Every follower of Christ has a personal responsibility to obey Christ's instructions to stay awake, be alert, on guard and keeping watch.

Pastors were sleeping too!

However, to those who have been given leadership responsibility in the household of God, they will be held to a higher accountability. In Matthew 24:45-51, Christ warned those He left in charge of His household, that He would cut them to pieces if they did not provide the food (Word) at the proper time (Time of the End).

> "Who then is the faithful and wise servant, whom the master has put **in charge of the servants in his household** to give them their food at the proper time? … But suppose **that servant is wicked** and says to himself, **'My master is staying away a long time.'** (Matthew 24:45-48)

Those assigned as watchmen who were the pastors, priests and shepherds in God's household did not provide the Word at the proper time. Therefore, the Household of God remained asleep for over ten years after the Time of the End had begun in 2001.

Yahweh prophesied about the Time of the End shepherds. Below is what Isaiah wrote:

> "**Israel's watchmen are blind**, they all lack knowledge; they are all mute dogs, they cannot bark; they lie around and dream, they love to sleep. They are dogs with mighty appetites; they never have enough. **They are shepherds who lack understanding**; they all turn to their own way, each seeks his own gain." (Isaiah 56:10-11)

God also explained that the churches would be asleep when the Time of the End began. Some of this will certainly be as a result of the pastors' blindness and lack of understanding. Christ explained this in the parable of the Ten Virgins. At the Time of the End all the churches would be asleep. Here is how he described this End Time situation in Matthew 25:

> "At that time the kingdom of heaven will be like ten virgins [church] who took their lamps and went out to meet the bridegroom. ... The bridegroom was a long time in coming, and **they all became drowsy and fell asleep**. At midnight **the cry rang out**: 'Here comes the bridegroom! Come out to meet him!' Then **all the virgins woke up** and trimmed their lamps." (Matthew 24:1-7)

Notice in this parable that Christ indicated that at first all those who are waiting for Christ would be asleep, **all of them**. Then a cry rang out and all of them woke up. It will be just like this when the Second Seal of Revelation is opened. **A cry will ring out and all the churches will wake up** to the realization that the Time of the End Has Come and the End of the Age is near.

Note: The wake up cry, the cry that wakes up all the churches, is recorded below.

> "The sound of **a cry comes from Babylon**, the sound of great destruction from the land of the Babylonians." (Jeremiah 51:54)

Now let's examine the Second Seal prophecy and find out what it is that will wake up all the sleeping churches.

What we now know:

- Horses symbolize armies and their riders their leaders.
- Where God assigned the four horses of Revelation.
- That the First Seal prophecy has been fulfilled.
- The churches are still asleep. But not for long.

Red Horse and Rider

Now, we will examine Revelation's Second Seal Horse and Rider and discuss why this prophecy is so important to Yahweh's people.

When Christ opens the second seal the rider on the red horse will take peace from the earth, start world war. It will be the Second Seal war and crisis which will finally awaken all the churches to the fact that the Time of the End has come.

Now, here is how the second seal prophecy is described in most English Bibles:

> "When the Lamb opened the second seal, I heard the second living creature say, "Come!" Then another horse came out, a fiery red one. **Its rider was given power to take peace from the earth** and to make men slay each other. **To him was given a large sword.**" (Revelation 6:3-4)

As we read in Zechariah 6, the red horse is one of the four spirits of heaven that has gone out from the presence of the Lord of the whole world. Zechariah's prophecy indicates that the white horses were assigned to the West and the red horses to the East.

Rider on the Red Horse

Now that the First Seal has been opened and fulfilled we know that the Second Seal prophecy is the next seal to be opened and fulfilled. A leader and his military from the East of Israel will start world war.

Let's take another look at our map of Zechariah's four horses. The map indicates where the colored horses were assigned by God, based on Zechariah chapter six.

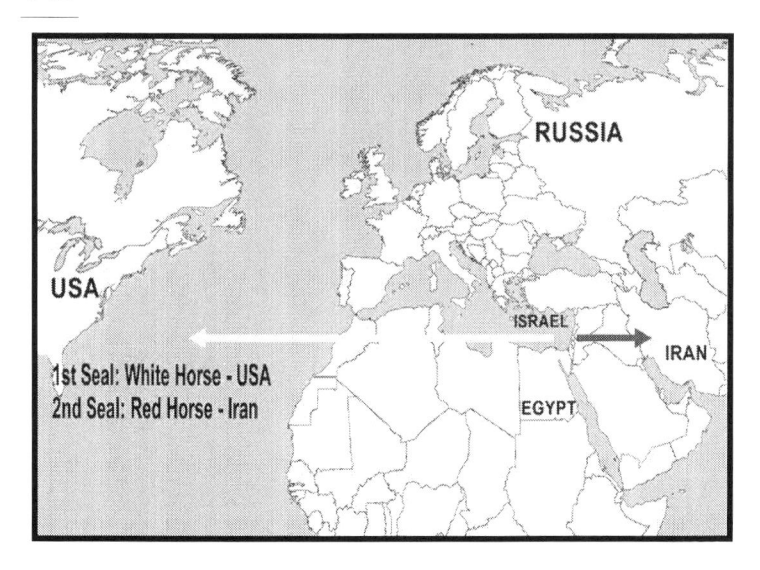

We are told that the second seal leader will be "given power to take peace from the earth and to make men slay each other." Therefore, the opening of the second seal will mark the beginning of world war.

When the second seal opens, war on earth will have reached a new level, going from regional conflicts to global. The major world powers like Russia, China, the United States and others will begin to openly oppose each other in a global struggle.

The second seal will mark the beginning of this global conflict in the Time of the End. It does not mark the end itself. Many prophecies remain to be fulfilled before the End of the Age. This Second Seal war will last for years before the Third Seal is opened.

Bible prophecy seems to indicate that nuclear weapons will be used at the time of the Second Seal war and will then be used again on a much larger scale in the Third Seal war.

The Second Seal war will likely be a World War.

How will the Second Seal war begin?

World War

In the Second Seal prophecy, after we were told that peace is taken from the earth we were told that the rider on the red horse would be given a large sword. Let's examine exactly how this prophecy is written:

> "To him was given a large [megas] sword [machaira]." (Revelation" 6:4)

This seems to indicate **how** the leader from the East will take peace from the earth.

Since militaries today do not use large swords, let's examine the original Greek words which are translated "large sword." The Greek words can help us determine what the prophecy means in the context of modern warfare.

The Greek words for "large sword" are 'megas' and 'machaira'.

> 'Megas' means; large, **great**, loud or mighty.

'Machaira' means; sword and it comes from the root word 'mache' meaning **battle**, controversy or fight.

In modern terms the second seal prophecy seems to indicate that the rider on the red horse will take peace from the earth with either "**a great battle**" or "**a mighty weapon**."

Second Seal Prophecy Fulfilled

Before we consider the rider on the red horse, let me point out that this second seal prophecy will be the second major Time of the End prophecy to be fulfilled.

This second major End Time prophecy will also serve as a second prophetic witness to the Time of the End.

> "Every matter must be established by the testimony of two or three witnesses." (2 Corinthians 13:1)

When the second seal prophecy is fulfilled we will have the second witness to the End Time and be able to scripturally establish that the Time of the End has come.

It's 2013 and over ten years have passed since the first seal was opened on 9/11. Based on what Christ said about the Time of the End being less than a generation, we must be getting very close to when the Second Seal will be opened.

If God has told us everything, then He must have already indicated for us who the Red Horse will be.

He has, the Red Horse symbolizes IRAN!

IRAN will fulfill the Second Seal Prophecy

How do I know that Iran is the country that will be taking peace from the earth? There are three reasons:

First, I have already explained how I was led by Yahweh to understand the symbolism of Revelation's first four seals.

That the "horses and riders" symbolize "armies and their leaders" and that the "four colored horses" symbolize the countries which will start each of the first four seal wars, like the U.S. started the War on Terror.

Second, in September of 2009, the Lord spoke to me in the spirit and said, "**The red horse symbolizes Iran. I have stirred up the kings of the Medes because my purpose is to destroy Babylon.**"

The Lord's statement told to me in the Spirit, showed me from Scripture that Iran will fulfill the Second Seal prophecy.

The first sentence of what He said, "The red horse symbolizes Iran" stated who the Second Seal country is.

Third, the second sentence of what He said I later identified as a prophecy which Yahweh had previously given to Jeremiah regarding the End Time Babylonians. Here is what Yahweh told Jeremiah about Babylon:

> "Sharpen the arrows, take up the shields! **Yahweh has stirred up the kings of the Medes, because his purpose is to destroy Babylon**. Yahweh will take vengeance, vengeance for his temple. Lift up a banner against the walls of Babylon! Reinforce the guard, station the watchmen, **prepare an ambush**! Yahweh will carry out his purpose, his decree against the people of Babylon. You who live by many waters and are rich in treasures, your end has come, the time for you to be cut off." (Jeremiah 51:11-13)

Here is what this passage means to me and why it confirms to me that Iran is the Red Horse of Revelation.

- The ancient Medes are ancestors of the Iranians.

- I know from Revelation 17 and Daniel 8 and 11 that the Antichrist will get credit for destroying End Time Babylon. Since, the Antichrist does not come from Iran this prophecy must be describing something that Iran will do that leads to Babylon's destruction, not the destruction itself.

- The word that Yahweh gave me regarding Iran fits perfectly like a piece in a puzzle. The puzzle is a large prophetic picture that God has provided regarding the Time of the End. Iran fits!

Before we move on, let's update our timeline with the 2nd Seal war.

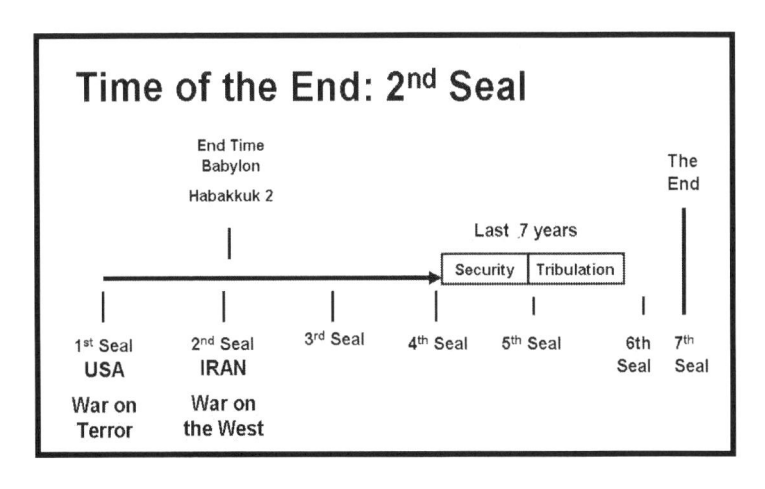

Time of the End: 2nd Seal

1st Seal	2nd Seal	3rd Seal	4th Seal	5th Seal	6th Seal	7th Seal
USA	IRAN					
War on Terror	War on the West					

End Time Babylon — Habakkuk 2 (at 2nd Seal)

Last 7 years: Security | Tribulation

The End (at 7th Seal)

Now, let's review another aspect of the Second Seal prophecy.

After the two witnesses

When we have seen the fulfillment of the first two seal prophecies of Revelation we will have heard from two scriptural witnesses confirming that the Time of the End has come. The Bible says it takes two or three witnesses to establish a matter.

Yahweh has also provided a third prophetic witness so we can be absolutely certain! After all, confirming that we are in the Time of the End is extremely important to Yahweh's people and He would not leave us with just two witnesses.

Only Yahweh knows exactly what will happen and when. However, He has given us these prophecies so that we can be alert, on guard and keeping watch.

As we know, before the Second Seal opened Yahweh's people were all asleep. However, when they all awake to the realization that the Time of the End has come, many things will change.

Let's discuss one of those changes before we move on and consider the third witness and its impact on Yahweh's people.

All the churches wake up.

We should also be aware that it was Christ who strongly warned His Church not to sleep. Here is what He said,

"Be on guard! Be alert! You do not know when that time will come.... Therefore keep watch ... If he comes suddenly, **do not let him find you sleeping.** What I say to you, I say to everyone: 'Watch!'" (Mark 13:33-37)

Let's look at a couple of His warnings in Revelation,

"Remember, therefore, what you have received and heard; obey it, and repent. But **if you do not wake up**, I will come like a thief, and you will not know at what time I will come to you." (Revelation 3:3)

"Behold, I come like a thief! **Blessed is he who stays awake.**" (Revelation 16:15)

We can clearly see that Christ wanted His Church to be awake! However, He also knew that they would **all** fall asleep as we have read in the "parable of the Ten Virgins" in Matthew 25:1-7.

He also warned the pastors that there would be dire consequences if they failed to follow His instructions. Here is an excerpt from that warning,

> "If the owner of the house had known at what time of night the thief was coming, he would have kept watch and would not have let his house be broken into. ... Who then is the faithful and wise servant, **whom the master has put in charge of the servants in his household** to give them their food at the proper time? ... But suppose that servant is wicked and says to himself, 'My master is staying away a long time,' ... The master of that servant will come on a day when he does not expect him and ... cut him to pieces and assign him a place with the hypocrites, where there will be weeping and gnashing of teeth." (Matthew 24:43-51)

God also foretold that the shepherds would be caught off guard by the coming Time of the End. For example:

> "Israel's watchmen are blind, **they all lack knowledge**; they are all mute dogs, they cannot bark; they lie around and dream, they love to sleep. ... They are **shepherds who lack understanding; they all turn to their own way**, each seeks his own gain." (Isaiah 56:10-11)

Yahweh is not pleased with the shepherds who where in charge when the Time had come. Here is what He said through Ezekiel,

> "This is what the Sovereign **Yahweh says: I am against the shepherds and will hold them accountable** for my flock. I will remove them from tending the flock so that the shepherds can no longer feed themselves. I will rescue my flock from their mouths, and it will no longer be food for them. ... I myself will search for my sheep and look after them." (Ezekiel 34:10-11)

There will be consequences for the shepherds as well as the flock for not staying wake and being alert to the Time of the End. All Yahweh's people should have been in their Bibles, understanding about the Second Coming and keeping watch. If they had, they would have been able to identify Revelation's First Seal prophecy years earlier and been ready for the **Second Seal war** and **the economic crisis that would follow.**

Never the less, God knew this would happen. That is why He planned to wake them all at the Second Seal. At the Second Seal **there is still time** for the Church! **But, no time to lose**!

Now that we have covered the Second Seal prophecy we are ready to examine the Third Seal prophecy.

Chapter 9

Seal Wars with Antichrist

As Birth Pains

Before we examine the black horse and rider of Revelation's Third Seal, we should remember that we are examining prophecies which Christ called "birth pains." Birth pains in pregnancy start small and increase in severity. Just as the Second Seal war will be larger than the first, the Third Seal war will be larger than the second. Also, like birth pains the Third Seal crisis will follow more quickly than did the second.

As we have just seen, Revelations first two seal prophecies do not involve the Antichrist. He will begin to arise soon after the ten nations come together, following Revelation's Second Seal War. From then on the Antichrist will be involved in all the Time of the End Wars, beginning with Revelation's Third Seal War.

We will now pick up with Revelation's Third Seal Prophecy.

Black Horse and Rider

Now we will examine Revelation's Third Seal horse and rider and discuss why this prophecy is extremely important to God's people, a matter of life and death to many.

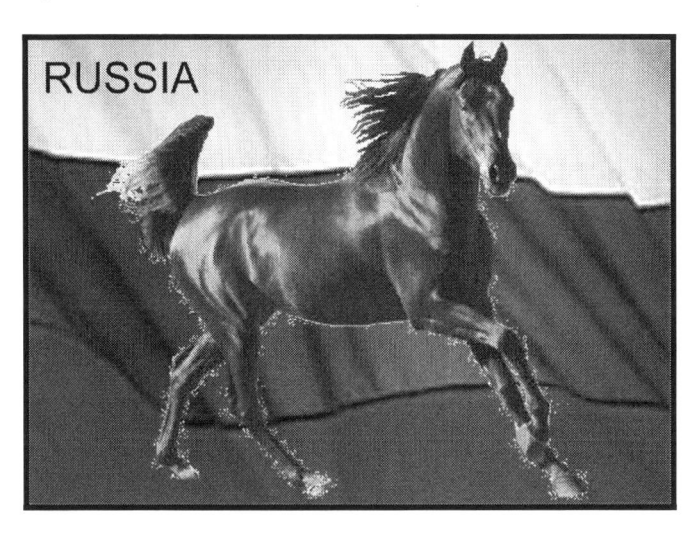

When Christ opens the third seal it appears that the rider on the black horse will cause damage to the world's supply of wheat and barley. Below, is Revelation's Third Seal prophecy.

> "When the Lamb opened **the third seal**, I heard the third living creature say, "Come!" I looked, and there before me was a black horse! **Its rider was holding a pair of scales** in his hand. Then I heard what sounded like a voice among the four living creatures, saying, "A quart of wheat for a day's wages, and three quarts of barley for a day's wages, and do not damage the oil and the wine!" (Revelation 6:5-6)

At least one word in this translation may be worth examining more closely. The Greek word which is translated "**pair of scales**" is "zugos." Zugos; means a beam of a balance (as connecting scales). Therefore, the rider on the black horse may have something to do with balance in the world, like the balance of power. Since each of the riders seems to start wars, this rider may start a war that will alter the balance of power for the whole world.

There is another aspect to this prophecy that also seems to connote war. It says "do not damage the oil and the wine!" This implies that wheat and barley will be damaged causing a sharp rise in the price of wheat and barley.

Zechariah's Map of the Four Colored Horses

Let's get some geographic perspective of the Black Horse from our world map of the four colored horses below.

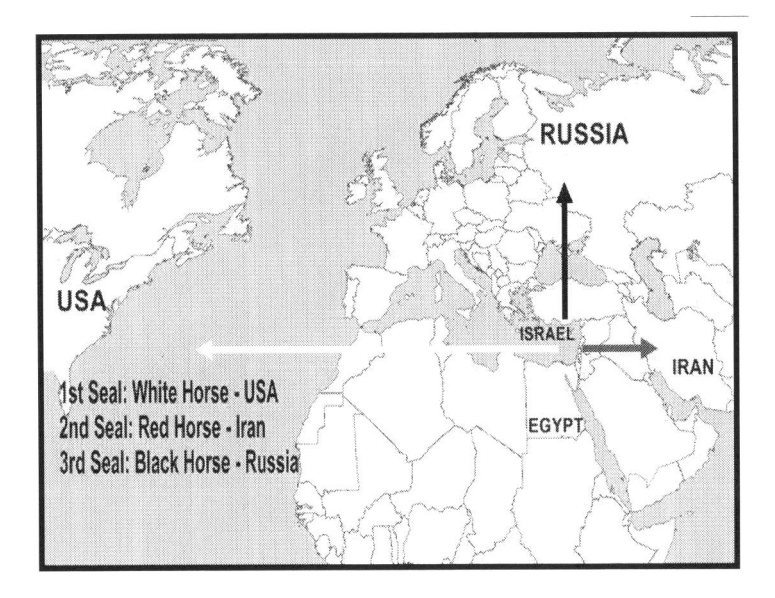

As we can see, Russia is the country north of Israel capable of starting this Third Seal war.

Wheat and Barley Damaged

When this war takes place it appears that wheat and barley are damaged causing a dramatic rise in the price of wheat and barley. After the wheat and barley are damaged it will cost a day's wages to buy a day's supply of wheat or barley bread.

Today, the United States of America and Canada combined typically represent the top world exporters of wheat and barley.[4] The U.S.A. and Canada together provide about 40% of global wheat exports.

4

http://www.abareconomics.com/interactive/08_ResearchReports/gmcr

Secondly, Russia has for several years been rebuilding its strategic nuclear capabilities.[5] Some believe that under the leadership of Vladimir Putin, the Russian Bear has awakened and has revived its Cold War strategies.

If Russia attacks the United States, the United States would likely be able to counter attack and cause significant devastation to Russia. Russia also is a major producer of wheat. Therefore, if Russia were to engage the U.S. in a thermo nuclear war, wheat and barley would very likely reach the cost described in the Third Seal prophecy.

Babylon the Great, a.k.a. the U.S.A.

We have already begun to consider the End Time Babylonians. But, now in light of the Third Seal horse and rider we need to take a closer look. We must be absolutely certain who the Babylonians are because Yahweh has already warned His people to leave Babylon the Great before it's too late.

---

ops/htm/chapter_3.htm

[5]

http://online.wsj.com/article/SB121928439171059051.html?mod=googlenews_wsj

Yahweh has commanded that His people flee from the land of the Babylonians before she is attacked. Since it appears that Russia is the nation from the north that will attack the U.S.A. we should also be able to confirm this in other prophecies about End Time Babylon. Because of the critical nature of Babylon's identity for Yahweh's people, we would be wise to apply the "two or three witnesses" rule.

Since Jeremiah wrote extensively about the End Time Babylonians, let's start with his prophecies. According to Jeremiah who is it that will attack the Babylonians?

> "This is the word Yahweh spoke through Jeremiah the prophet concerning Babylon and the land of the Babylonians: Announce and proclaim among the nations, lift up a banner and proclaim it; keep nothing back… **A nation from the north will attack her** and lay waste her land." (Jeremiah 50:1-3)

This next passage from Jeremiah seems to capture several important aspects concerning Babylon's defeat including God's command for His people to flee from Babylon.

> "**Flee out of Babylon;** leave the land of the Babylonians, and be like the goats that lead the flock. For I will stir up and bring against Babylon **an alliance of great nations from the land of the north**. They will take up their positions against her, and **from the north** she will be captured. **Their arrows will be like skilled warriors** who do not return empty-handed. So Babylonia will be plundered." (Jeremiah 50:8-10)

Yahweh tells us that End Time Babylon will be defeated by fire in a moment by a nation from the north along with an alliance of other nations. It's also interesting that this destruction comes as "their arrows will be like skilled warriors." Arrows are weapons of war that fly through the air. In ancient times it was the archers that were the skilled warriors. Today ICBM's are programmed to operate like skilled warriors and evade detection and interception by antimissile missile systems.

Some people have the mistaken idea that Old Testament prophets only wrote about the past. That is far from the truth. The prophets actually give Yahweh's people, today, more about their future than does the New Testament. For example, here is something that has never happened in the past. You can expect it in the future.

> "**As God overthrew Sodom and Gomorrah** along with their neighboring towns," declares Yahweh, "so no one will live there; no man will dwell in it. "Look! **An army is coming from the north**; a **great nation and many kings** are being stirred up from the ends of the earth." (Jeremiah 50:40-41)

From history, we know that these prophecies are not about ancient Babylon. Ancient Babylon gradually faded away over many decades. She was not destroyed by fire in one hour and day as End Time Babylon will be. Let's examine this one day and one hour destruction by fire with other prophesies before we move on.

Isaiah wrote about End Time Babylon:

> "**Babylon**, the jewel of kingdoms, the glory of the Babylonians' pride, **will be overthrown by God like Sodom and Gomorrah.**" (Isaiah 13:19)

John also wrote of the destruction of End Time Babylon in the Book of Revelation which we will also discuss later in chapter 11.

> "The beast [Antichrist] and the ten horns you saw will hate the prostitute. They will bring her to ruin and leave her naked; they will eat her flesh and **burn her with fire**. For God has put it into their hearts to accomplish his purpose." (Revelation 17:16-17)

> "Therefore **in one day** her plagues will overtake her: death, mourning and famine. **She will be consumed by fire**, for mighty is the Lord God who judges her. When the kings of the earth who committed adultery with her and shared her luxury see the smoke of her burning, they will weep and mourn over her. Terrified at her torment, they will stand far off and cry: 'Woe! Woe, O great city, O Babylon, city of power! **In one hour your doom has come**!' The merchants of the earth will weep and mourn over her because **no one** buys their cargoes any more." (Revelation 18:8-11)

How End Time Babylon is destroyed is no mystery! When she is destroyed by fire in one day and one hour the world wide economy stops because the world's great consumer nation is gone. What other nation could possibly cause "The merchants of the earth will weep and mourn over her because **no one buys their cargoes any more**"?

What about the wheat and barley destruction mentioned in the Third Seal prophecy? Do we see anything about this when the Land of the Babylonians is destroyed? Jeremiah says this about that.

> "Cut off from Babylon the sower, and the reaper with his sickle at harvest." (Jeremiah 50:16)

> "Come against her from afar. Break open her granaries; pile her up like heaps of grain. Completely destroy her and leave her no remnant." (Jeremiah 50:26)

Awake Yet?

Hopefully, by now, everyone is seeing why Yahweh is telling His people to leave the land and the city of the End Time Babylonians before it is too late.

Yahweh's warning for His people to "**come out**" was one of the reasons I was able to see that the "Parable of the Ten Virgins" awakening will happen as a result of Revelation's Second Seal War. I reasoned that if there was any hope of God's people getting the message to leave Babylon before its destruction, His people would have to be awake for some time before that happened.

In the Matthew 25 parable, there are a couple of clues that alert us to the fact that the awakening of the "ten virgins" is before Babylon's destruction at the Third Seal War.

The first clue:

At the time of the parable, Christ said the virgins were told to "**come out**" to meet Him.

> "At midnight the cry rang out: 'See, the bridegroom is coming! "**Come out**" (exerchomai) to meet him!' Then all the virgins woke up." (Matthew 25:6-7)

The word in the Greek translated "**come out**" is "exerchomai."

> Exerchomai means to come out, depart (out of), escape, get out, go (abroad, away, out).

This same word is used in exactly the same context in Christ's warning to His people in Revelation 18:4 as we read below regarding "Babylon the Great."

"**Come out** (exerchomai) of her, my people, so that you will not share in her sins, so that you will not receive any of her plagues." (Revelation 18:4)

The Second Clue:

At the time of the parable a cry is heard.

> "At midnight **the cry rang out**: 'See, the bridegroom is coming! "Come out to meet him!' Then all the virgins woke up." (Matthew 25:6-7)

That cry, at the time of the Second Seal War, is the same cry that Jeremiah said would come from the Babylonians.

> "**The sound of a cry** comes from Babylon, the sound of great destruction from the land of the Babylonians. Yahweh will destroy Babylon; ... A destroyer will come against Babylon." (Jeremiah 51:54-56)

When Yahweh's people wake up and turn to the Bible, they will see why they must "come out" of Babylon before it is too late. This may be a good time to take a look at our 3rd Seal timeline.

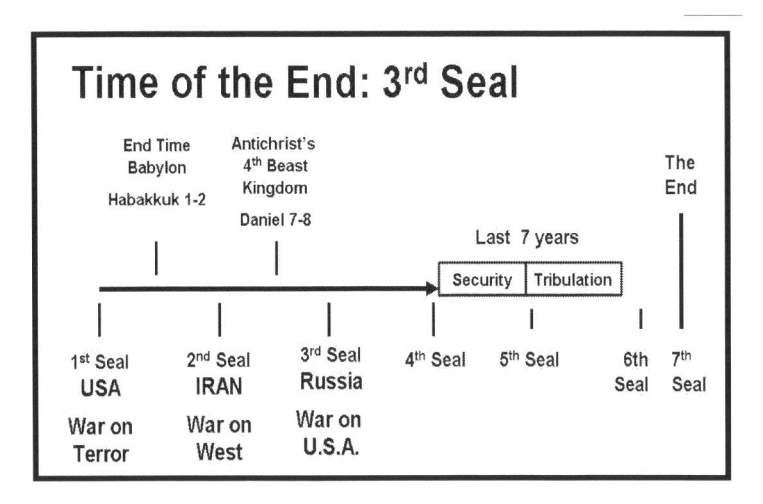

```
Time of the End: 3rd Seal

End Time          Antichrist's
Babylon           4th Beast                                    The
                  Kingdom                                      End
Habakkuk 1-2
                  Daniel 7-8
                                        Last 7 years
                                     ┌──────────┬──────────┐
                                     │ Security │Tribulation│
                                     └──────────┴──────────┘
  │         │         │         │         │         │    │
1st Seal  2nd Seal  3rd Seal  4th Seal  5th Seal  6th   7th
 USA       IRAN     Russia                        Seal  Seal

War on    War on    War on
Terror    West      U.S.A.
```

Soon after the Second Seal is opened, Yahweh's people will begin to realize that they need to leave Babylon before the Third Seal is opened. Then they will want to know **where Yahweh says to go**. The answer is found six times in Jeremiah 50-51. Below are two examples:

> "Listen to the fugitives and refugees from Babylon declaring **in Zion** (Jerusalem) how Yahweh our God has taken vengeance" (Jeremiah 50:28).

> "Yahweh has vindicated us; come, let us tell **in Zion** (Jerusalem) what Yahweh our God has done" (Jeremiah 51:10).

Pale Horse and Rider

Now we will examine Revelation's Fourth Seal horse and rider and discuss why this prophecy is important to God's people.

As we examine the pale horse and rider of Revelation's Fourth Seal. We will also consider several other prophecies that will also be fulfilled at the time of the Fourth Seal. These prophecies will identify the pale horse country by name and help us see when this Fourth Seal war will occur.

Let's start by examining the Fourth Seal prophecy.

> "I looked, and there before me was a pale horse! Its rider was named Death, and Hades was following close behind him. They were given power over a fourth of the earth to kill by sword, famine and plague, and by the wild beasts of the earth." (Revelation 6:8)

As we consider the Fourth Seal prophecy there are several things that we need to keep in mind. First, where to look for the pale horse and rider? Let's start with Zechariah's Map of the Four Colored Horses.

The Four Colored Horses of Zechariah 6

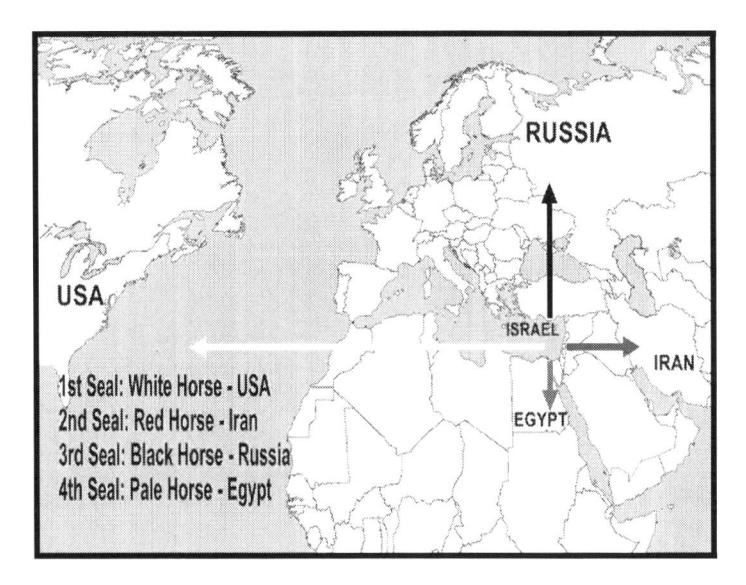

Map showing USA, Russia, Israel, Iran, and Egypt with arrows indicating directions of conflict.

1st Seal: White Horse - USA
2nd Seal: Red Horse - Iran
3rd Seal: Black Horse - Russia
4th Seal: Pale Horse - Egypt

South of Israel is Egypt and that is where we will need to watch when it's time for the Fourth Seal war to start.

A second thing we need to keep in mind is that the Fourth Seal war is a "birth pain" which means it will come quickly after the Third Seal war and be more severe than any of the three previous wars.

The idea that this will be a bigger war seems to be born out by the prophecy itself when it says, "**They were given power over a fourth of the earth** to kill." Whether "a fourth of the earth" refers to land mass or world population we can see that this war will be very large indeed.

Remember how we used other End Time prophecies to confirm that the Third Seal black horse from the north symbolized Russia? Let's do the same with the pale horse from the south to see what the prophets say.

The prophet Daniel has a prophecy that tells us several things about the Fourth Seal war. Let's see what we can learn from Daniel.

King of the South

The first thing we see in Daniel 11:39 is that the Antichrist attacks "the mightiest fortresses." This has something to do with the Third Seal war we examined previously. When the Third Seal is opened the US superpower will be destroyed as a nation.

After that the king of the South, Egypt, will engage the Antichrist in battle. The king of the South is the Fourth Seal rider on the pale horse. Therefore, the timing of this war in Daniel 11 is after the Third Seal war and it corresponds exactly with Revelation's Fourth Seal war.

> "He [Antichrist] will attack **the mightiest fortresses** with the help of a foreign god and will greatly honor those who acknowledge him. ... At the time of the end the **king of the South** will engage him [Antichrist] in battle, and the king of the North will storm out against him with chariots and cavalry and a great fleet of ships. He [Antichrist] will invade many countries and sweep through them like a flood. He [Antichrist] will also invade the Beautiful Land. … He [Antichrist] will extend his power over many countries; Egypt will not escape. He [Antichrist] will gain control of the treasures of gold and silver and all the riches of Egypt, with the Libyans and Nubians in submission." (Daniel 11:39-43)

There are still some other very interesting things revealed in this prophecy that we should know.

After "the king of the South" (Egypt) engages the Antichrist in battle, the Antichrist "invades the Beautiful Land" (Israel).

We know from prophecy that Israel is the "Beautiful Land" because of Daniel 11:16 which also refers to the "Beautiful Land," was fulfilled in 200 B.C. in a battle between Antiochus III and Ptolemy V Epiphanes.[6]

Antichrist in Israel

---

[6] http://www.bibleexplained.com/prophets/daniel/da11.htm

Daniel's prophecy places the Antichrist in Israel just after the Fourth Seal war. By this time there will have already been a covenant made for Israel's peace. It is likely that the Antichrist will want to regroup and consolidate his power following the huge war he has just fought. Therefore, rather than engage Israel in battle, he will likely decide to confirm the existing covenant with them and return home to Iraq.

This will mark the beginning of the last seven years, the 70th 'seven' of Daniel chapter nine.

> "He [Antichrist] will confirm a covenant with many for one 'seven.' In the middle of the 'seven' he will put an end to sacrifice and offering. And on a wing of the temple he will set up an abomination that causes desolation." (Daniel 9:27)

There is still more. Daniel's prophecy identifies three of the 10 nations that will initially comprise the Kingdom of the Antichrist. Two of the nations' names have remained to this day while the third is identified by the name of its ancient tribe. Therefore, three of the ten nations will be Egypt, Libya and Sudan. The ancient Nubians were from the territory of Sudan.[7]

> "Egypt, with the Libyans and Nubians **[three] in submission.**" (Daniel 11:43)

---

[7] http://en.wikipedia.org/wiki/Nubia

This is an amazing revelation which actually identifies three of the ten nations of the Antichrist's kingdom, two of them by name. It also agrees with Daniel 7 which describes how the Kingdom of the Antichrist will arise to power.

Let's look at the connection between these three nations named in Daniel 11 and in Daniel 7 below.

> "The fourth beast is a fourth kingdom that will appear on earth. It will be different from all the other kingdoms and will devour the whole earth, trampling it down and crushing it. The ten horns are ten kings who will come from this kingdom. After them another king [Antichrist] will arise, different from the earlier ones; **he will subdue three kings.**" (Daniel 7:23-24)

Yahweh also told Daniel about this breakup of the Kingdom of the Antichrist in Daniel chapter two. Let's read what Daniel wrote:

> "**Finally, there will be a fourth kingdom,** strong as iron--for iron breaks and smashes everything--and as iron breaks things to pieces, so **it will crush and break all the others**. ... so **this kingdom will be partly strong and partly brittle**. And just as you saw the iron mixed with baked clay, so the people will be a mixture **and will not remain united**, any more than iron mixes with clay." (Daniel 2:40-43)

Now we know that the Middle Eastern Kingdom of the Antichrist will break up when the Fourth Seal is opened.

Let's take a look at our timeline to see where the 4th Seal will happen.

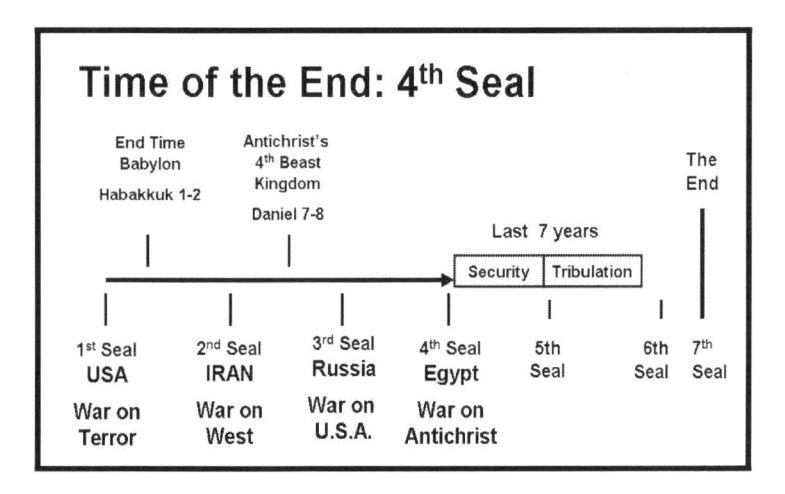

Time of the End: 4th Seal

			Last 7 years			
End Time Babylon Habakkuk 1-2	Antichrist's 4th Beast Kingdom Daniel 7-8		Security | Tribulation			The End
1st Seal USA War on Terror	2nd Seal IRAN War on West	3rd Seal Russia War on U.S.A.	4th Seal Egypt War on Antichrist	5th Seal	6th Seal	7th Seal

Some of you may be aware that this prophetic revelation is new. We should not be surprised by this, because Yahweh already told us that this would happen.

Unsealed and Opened at the appointed Time

In the Torah Yahweh warned His people about the End and indicated that He was keeping some prophecy in reserve. Here is what Yahweh said over 3,500 years ago.

> "They are a nation without sense, there is no discernment in them. If only they were wise and would understand this and discern what their **end will be**! ... Have I not **kept this in reserve** and <u>sealed</u> it in my vaults?" (Deuteronomy 32:28-34)

Daniel received a similar message from Yahweh indicating that the word would be sealed until the Time of the End had come. Here is what Yahweh told Daniel.

> "Go your way, Daniel, because the words are closed up and **sealed until the time of the end.**" (Daniel 12:9)

Now, that the Time has come, it should not be surprising to us that Revelation's Seals are revealing what has been "**sealed**" – new information that has been hidden in plain sight all this time.

Christ also said something that fits this when He was telling His disciples about the Time of the End. He indicated that no one would be able to know when the Time of the End was going to begin. Christ said,

> "Watch out that you are not deceived. For many will come in my name, claiming, 'I am he,' and, **'The time is near**.' Do not follow them." (Luke 21:8)

No one could possibly have known what the First Seal prophecy meant until after it was opened and unsealed by the Messiah. Then, and only then, would God's people be able to recognize that the First Seal prophecy had been fulfilled and that "The Time Has Come."

Now that we know that "the Time" has come and the End is near, let's see what happens after the four horsemen of Revelation.

The Fifth Seal of Revelation

The fifth seal of Revelation breaks from the pattern of 'horses and riders" and gives us a view of what is happening in heaven when the fifth seal is opened. Here is what John saw,

> "When he opened **the fifth seal**, I saw under the altar the souls of those who had been slain because of the word of God and the testimony they had maintained. They called out in a loud voice, "How long, Sovereign Lord, holy and true, until you judge the inhabitants of the earth and avenge our blood?" Then each of them was given a white robe, and they were told to wait a little longer, until the number of their fellow servants and brothers who were to be killed as they had been was completed." (Revelation 6:9-11)

Since this heavenly vision follows the Fourth Seal war and precedes the Sixth Seal war, it will likely occur at the time of the Great Tribulation which begins in the middle of the last seven years of this age. The Great Tribulation, like the previous four seals is also a war. The Fifth Seal will likely be War on the Saints.

Here is where I would place the 5th Seal on our Time of the End timeline.

Time of the End: 5th Seal

End Time Babylon — Habakkuk 1-2	Antichrist's 4th Beast Kingdom — Daniel 7-8

Last 7 years: Security | Tribulation

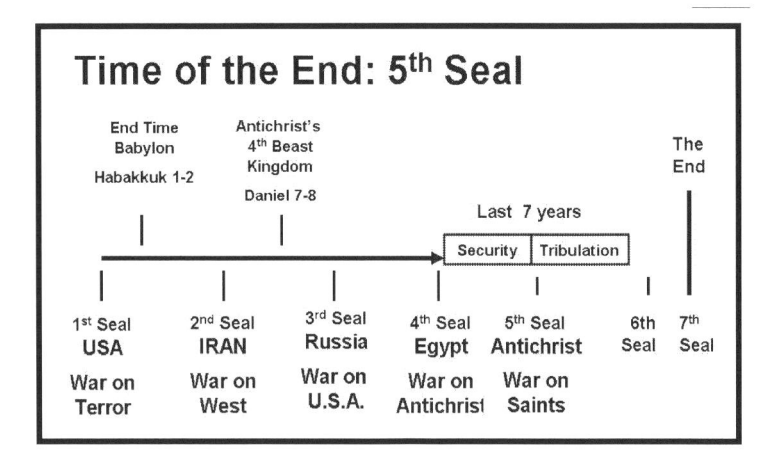

- 1st Seal — USA — War on Terror
- 2nd Seal — IRAN — War on West
- 3rd Seal — Russia — War on U.S.A.
- 4th Seal — Egypt — War on Antichrist
- 5th Seal — Antichrist — War on Saints
- 6th Seal
- 7th Seal — The End

Next to be opened by the Messiah is the Sixth Seal of the Scroll.

Sixth Seal of Revelation

The Sixth Seal is much easier to place on our timeline, because the prophecy gives us some Scriptural reference points. First let's look at the Sixth Seal prophecy as it is written.

"I watched as he opened **the sixth seal**. There was a great earthquake. **The sun turned black like sackcloth made of goat hair, the whole moon turned blood red, and the stars in the sky fell to earth**, as late figs drop from a fig tree when shaken by a strong wind. The sky receded like a scroll, rolling up, and every mountain and island was removed from its place. Then the kings of the earth, the princes, the generals, the rich, the mighty, and every slave and every free man hid in caves and among the rocks of the mountains. They called to the mountains and the rocks, "Fall on us and hide us from the face of him who sits on the throne and from the wrath of the Lamb! For the great day of their wrath has come, and who can stand?" (Revelation 6:12-17)

The Sixth Seal prophecy reveals some important things about the timing of the Second Coming, some things you may not have heard before.

First, let's get a visual perspective from our timeline.

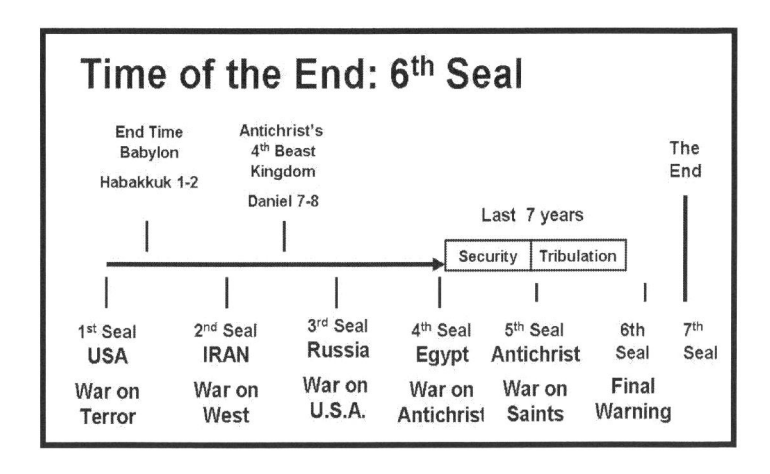

Time of the End: 6th Seal

Seal	1st Seal	2nd Seal	3rd Seal	4th Seal	5th Seal	6th Seal	7th Seal
Power	USA	IRAN	Russia	Egypt	Antichrist		
Event	War on Terror	War on West	War on U.S.A.	War on Antichrist	War on Saints	Final Warning	

- End Time Babylon — Habakkuk 1-2
- Antichrist's 4th Beast Kingdom — Daniel 7-8
- Last 7 years: Security | Tribulation
- The End

The timeline indicates that the 6th Seal is opened after the Great Tribulation, but before the Seventh Seal and the Second Coming. How do we know that's true? Once again, we will know what is true, not based on what we have heard from Man, but from the Word of Yahweh. We will turn to Scripture to determine when the Sixth Seal is opened.

When the Sixth Seal opens "**The sun turned black like sackcloth made of goat hair, the whole moon turned blood red, and the stars in the sky fell to earth**." When does Scripture say these things will happen? Christ said these things would happen immediately after the Great Tribulation.

> "Immediately after the tribulation of those days '**the sun will be darkened, and the moon will not give its light; the stars will fall from the sky.**'" (Matthew 24:29)

The prophet Joel said these things would happen before the Day of Yahweh (the LORD). Here Joel describes these signs in the sun, moon and stars as taking place before Yahweh (the LORD) returns with His army.

> "**Before them** the earth shakes, **the sky trembles, the sun and moon are darkened, and the stars no longer shine**. Yahweh (the LORD) thunders at the head of his army; his forces are beyond number, and mighty are those who obey his command. The day of Yahweh (the LORD) is great; it is dreadful. Who can endure it?" (Joel 2:10-11)

Similarly, Joel describes these signs in the heavens and on earth as occurring before the Day of Yahweh (the LORD).

> "I will show wonders in the heavens and on the earth, blood and fire and billows of smoke. **The sun will be turned to darkness and the moon to blood <u>before</u>** the coming of **the great and dreadful day of Yahweh (the LORD).**" (Joel 2:30-31)

This sign in the sun, moon and stars is mentioned by several of the prophets, including Isaiah and Ezekiel, in connection to the coming Day of Yahweh. From the passages we just read from Matthew and Joel we are able to determine that the Six Seal will be opened just before the Second Coming of the Messiah – after the Tribulation and before the Day of the LORD.

Just as we see in our 6th Seal timeline, the 6th Seal opens after the Tribulation and before the End. When the Sixth Seal opens the Seventh Seal and the Second Coming will follow shortly.

Seventh Seal of Revelation

As we see the seven seals will span the "Time of the End" from the West's War on Terror to the Second Coming of Messiah.

Time of the End: 7th Seal

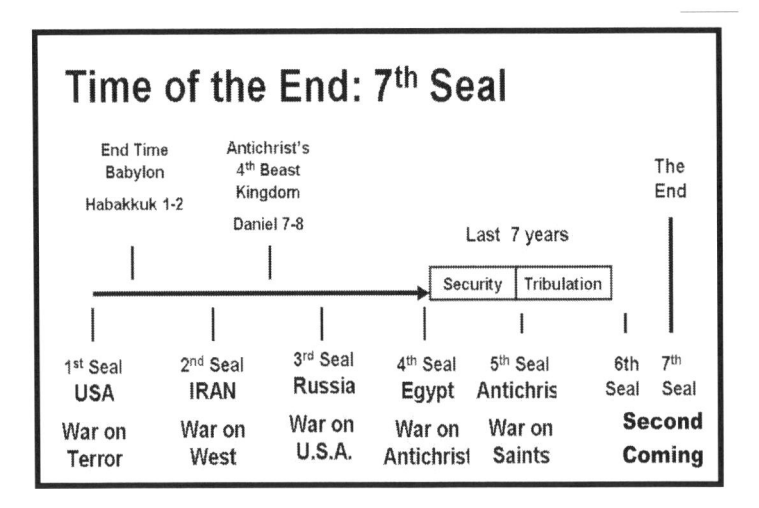

End Time Babylon Habakkuk 1-2	Antichrist's 4th Beast Kingdom Daniel 7-8			Last 7 years Security | Tribulation		The End
1st Seal **USA** War on Terror	2nd Seal **IRAN** War on West	3rd Seal **Russia** War on U.S.A.	4th Seal **Egypt** War on Antichrist	5th Seal **Antichris** War on Saints	6th Seal	7th Seal **Second Coming**

The Seventh Seal prophecy is very short and on the surface seems to reveal very little. However, in light of prophecy it reveals a great deal more than we've been told.

The Scroll of Life

Here is what Yahweh has revealed to me about the Scroll.

In the Bible we are told about the "Book of Life." The Book of life is the book that contains all the names of all Yahweh's people also known as the "Sons of God." The Book of life is mentioned in both the Old and New Testaments as we see below.

> "May they be blotted out of **the book (cipher) of life** and not be listed with the righteous." (Psalm 69:28)

The Hebrew word cipher is translated as "book" in Psalms **Cipher** means; writing, book, letter, register, scroll.

This means that in Hebrew, the book of life would also be the "Scroll of Life." As a matter of fact in those days books were scrolls since there were no books as we know them today.

This was also true at the time of Christ's first coming, books were actually scrolls. The "book of life' was also mentioned in the New Testament as we see below.

> "Yes, and I ask you, loyal yokefellow, help these women who have contended at my side in the cause of the gospel, along with Clement and the rest of my fellow workers, whose names are in **the book of life.**" (Philippians 4:3)

> "He who overcomes will, like them, be dressed in white. I will never blot out his name from **the book of life**, but will acknowledge his name before my Father and his angels." (Revelation 3:5)

The Greek word biblos is translated "book" in the New Testamant. Biblos means sheet, scroll, writing, book.

Now, let's compare these with the seven seal scroll.

> "Then I saw in the right hand of him who sat on the throne a scroll (biblion) with writing on both sides and sealed with seven seals." (Revelation 5:1)

The Greek word biblion (of the root biblos) means: roll, book, scroll, writing. Therefore, the "Book of Life" is synonymous with the "Scroll of Life."

Initially the Scroll was sealed with seven seals and could not be opened. But, after Christ removed the seventh seal the scroll could be opened and its contents revealed.

Here is how I envision the seven seal scroll.

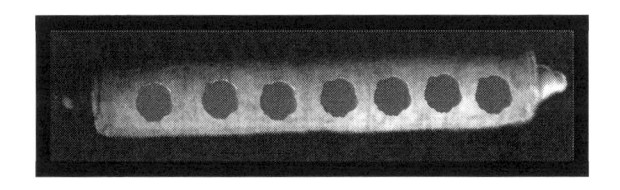

> "When he opened the seventh seal, there was silence in heaven for about half an hour" (Revelation 8:1).

What do the prophets say about the time when the Scroll will be opened? Isaiah was told this about the Scroll that would be opened at the Day of the LORD. Here is what he wrote.

> "Look in **the scroll of Yahweh** and read: **None of these will be missing**, not one will lack her mate. For it is his mouth that has given the order, and his Spirit **will gather them together**. He allots their portions; his hand distributes them by measure. **They will possess it forever and dwell there from generation to generation.**" (Isaiah 34:16-17)

In the New Testament we are told that all creation eagerly waits for the sons of God to be revealed.

> "Now if we are children, then we are heirs--heirs of God and co-heirs with Christ ... I consider that our present sufferings are not worth comparing with the glory that will be revealed in us. **The creation waits in eager expectation for the sons of God to be revealed.**" (Romans 8:17-19)

Perhaps this was why John was so upset when no one was found to open the scroll or even look inside it. Today, only Yahweh knows whose names are written in the Scroll of Life. Not even the angels know who the sons of God are. They too must wait for the Scroll to be opened. That is why Christ told them that they could not gather the wheat before the appointed time of the harvest.

> "When the wheat sprouted and formed heads, then the weeds also appeared. The owner's servants came to him and said, 'Sir, didn't you sow good seed in your field? Where then did the weeds come from?' An enemy did this,' he replied. The servants asked him, 'Do you want us to go and pull them up? '**No.**' he answered, '**because while you are pulling the weeds, you may root up the wheat with them. Let both grow together until the harvest**. At that time I will tell the harvesters: First collect the weeds and tie them in bundles to be burned; then gather the wheat and bring it into my barn.'" (Matthew 13:26-30)

When the Seventh Seal is opened and removed from the scroll, the scroll will be opened and the angels will then be able to know who Yahweh's people are. The angels will then gather them to the Lord in the air as He returns from heaven to earth to set up His Kingdom.

Now, let's get acquainted more with the Antichrist.

Chapter 10

More About Antichrist

> "The ten horns are ten kings who will come from this kingdom. After them another king will arise, different from the earlier ones;"
> Daniel 7:24

The Antichrist does not arise to power out of thin air, but arises to power from the fourth kingdom described in Daniel's prophesies. Therefore, we'll **first** examine the Middle East Kingdom of the Antichrist. **Second**, we'll see how Scripture describes the Antichrist himself. **Finally**, we will look at Revelation 13 which describes the Antichrist and his accomplice, the False Prophet.

I: Beast Kingdom

Daniel's prophecies point to the Antichrist arising out of the fourth and final kingdom. In Daniel 7 we are told that the fourth Kingdom will start with 10 kings. Then the Antichrist (another king) will arise among them. Here is how Daniel wrote this.

> "The fourth beast is a fourth kingdom that will appear on earth. It will be different from all the other kingdoms and will devour the whole earth, trampling it down and crushing it. **The ten horns are ten kings** who will come from this kingdom. **After them another king will arise**, different from the earlier ones; he will **subdue three kings.**" (Daniel 7:23-24)

As of June 2013 the ten kings (leaders) have not yet come together. They will come together after the Second Seal war of Revelation 6 but before the Third Seal war. When the ten nations unite we will see Daniel 7:24 partially fulfilled.

Note: In Daniel 7:24 above, for future reference, the kingdom starts out with 10 kings, then later 3 kings are subdued leaving 7 heads of state. When the 3 are subdued the kingdom will have "**seven heads and ten horns**."

From our discussion of the Fourth Seal war, we know that the Antichrist will subdue; Egypt, Libya and Sudan. Therefore, Egypt, Libya and Sudan will be three of the original ten kings.

What does Scripture tell us about the other seven? Who will they be?

There are several prophecies which indicate that the Antichrist will arise out of the Middle East and he will be from Iraq. Let's see what the prophets have to tell us.

Beast from the Middle East

Daniel's prophecies indicate that the fourth kingdom arises from the area of the first three Middle East kingdoms; Babylon, Media-Persia and Greece. Even Alexander the Great ruled his kingdom from the city of Babylon following his conquests. After Alexander conquered the known world from Greece to India, he returned to Babylon and governed from there. Alexander's capital Babylon was located on the Euphrates River south of present day Baghdad, in Iraq.

Now, let's look at how Isaiah described the Antichrist and his exploits.

> "Woe to the Assyrian, the rod of my anger, in whose hand is the club of my wrath!" (Isaiah 10:5)

> "When the Lord has finished all his work against Mount Zion and Jerusalem, he will say, "I will punish the king of Assyria for the willful pride of his heart and the haughty look in his eyes." (Isaiah 10:12)

Here is one of my favorite examples of how Isaiah identifies the Antichrist. Isaiah indicates that the Time of the End Assyrian king will come against Israel. The passage below indicates that Israel will first rely on the Antichrist. Then the Antichrist will strike them down until the end. Finally, the remnant of Israel, the survivors will truly rely on Yahweh. Here is how it is recorded:

> "In that day the remnant of Israel, the survivors of the house of Jacob, will no longer **rely on him** [King of Assyria] **who struck them down** but will truly **rely on Yahweh**, the Holy One of Israel." (Isaiah 10:20)

We know that the "King of Assyria" is the Antichrist, because Isaiah's description of the Antichrist matches perfectly with Daniel's description about the Antichrist. Here is Daniel's version:

> **"He [Antichrist] will confirm a covenant** with many for one 'seven.' In the middle of the 'seven' **he will put an end to sacrifice and offering**. And on a wing of the temple he will set up an abomination that causes desolation, **until the end."** (Daniel 9:27)

In both Daniel and Isaiah the Antichrist will at first provide for Israel's safety. Israel will rely on him. Then he will break the treaty, at the time of the "abomination that causes desolation," and he will "strike them down" during the Great Tribulation. The Great Tribulation will continue until about the time that the Messiah returns and saves His people from the Antichrist. Then they will truly rely on the Messiah, the Holy One of Israel.

In both prophecies the Antichrist will at first cause Israel to rely on him. Then he will beat them down during the Great Tribulation. At the end of the age, Yahweh will return and Israel will then rely on Him. Connecting these two key Time of the End prophecies, we can see that the Assyrian King is the Antichrist.

The prophet Isaiah was not the only prophet to identify the ruler who will come against Israel at the Time of the End. Micah also referred to the Antichrist as the Assyrian, as we see here:

> "He [Messiah] will stand and shepherd his flock in the strength of Yahweh, in the majesty of the name of Yahweh his God. And they [Israel] will live securely, for then his greatness will reach to the ends of the earth. And he will be their peace. When **the Assyrian** invades our land …" (Micah 5:4-5)

The prophet Zephaniah also wrote of Assyria as being the kingdom which will come against Israel during the Time of the End. Zephaniah further identified Assyria by referring to the Assyrian city of Nineveh. We can also be sure that this prophecy is about the end of the age and the Messiah's return, because Yahweh says "wait for me" and that the "whole world will be consumed by the fire." Let's read the prophecy:

> "He will stretch out his hand against the north and **destroy Assyria, leaving Nineveh utterly desolate** and dry as the desert.… 'Therefore wait for me,' declares Yahweh, for the day I will stand up to testify. I have decided to assemble the nations, to gather the kingdoms and to pour out my wrath on them-- all my fierce anger. The whole world will be consumed by the fire of my jealous anger." (Zephaniah 2:13, 3:8)

The prophet Nahum, like Zephaniah, referred to the city of Nineveh as the place of the Antichrist. Also like Zephaniah, Nahum indicates that Yahweh will totally destroy Nineveh in the end, as we read below:

> "**From you, O Nineveh, has one come** forth who plots evil against Yahweh and counsels wickedness. This is what Yahweh says: 'Although they have allies and are numerous, they will be cut off and pass away. Although I have afflicted you, O Judah, I will afflict you no more.' … Yahweh has given a command concerning you, Nineveh: 'You will have no descendants to bear your name.'" (Nahum 1:11-14)

As the prophets have written, the Antichrist will come from the land of ancient Assyria. **Ancient Assyria is present day Iraq**. Therefore, keep a close watch on Iraq as we wait for the fourth kingdom to form and the Antichrist to appear and begin his rise to world power.

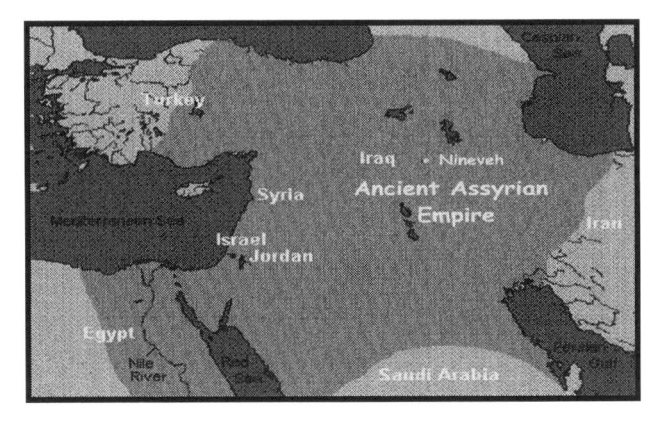

We are also told that the King of Assyria, Antichrist, will be successful until Yahweh returns. When the Messiah returns He will destroy the Antichrist who fought against Jerusalem, as we read here:

> "When the Lord has finished all his work against Mount Zion and Jerusalem, he will say, 'I will punish the king of Assyria [Antichrist] for the willful pride of his heart and the haughty look in his eyes.'" (Isaiah 10:12)

The Antichrist will come from present day Iraq. But, what other nations will be part of the 10 nation kingdom?

Turkey, one of the Ten

Ezekiel's prophecies indicate that Turkey will be one of the ten nations. In Ezekiel 38 and 39 we are told about the "**chief prince**" of several ancient territories which today are part of Turkey. The "chief prince" is the Antichrist and he will rule over the ten nations including Turkey. The nations of the Antichrist will ultimately gather and come against Jerusalem at the time of the Messiah's return, on the "Day of the Lord."

Below is a Hebrew map of the ancient territories mentioned in Ezekiel's prophecy. This map of the Black Sea region shows several of the territories mentioned in Ezekiel's prophecy about where the Antichrist "chief prince" will rule. If you look closely, you will see; Gomer, Magog, Togarmah, Meshech as well as other places mentioned in the Ezekiel 38:3-6 prophecy.

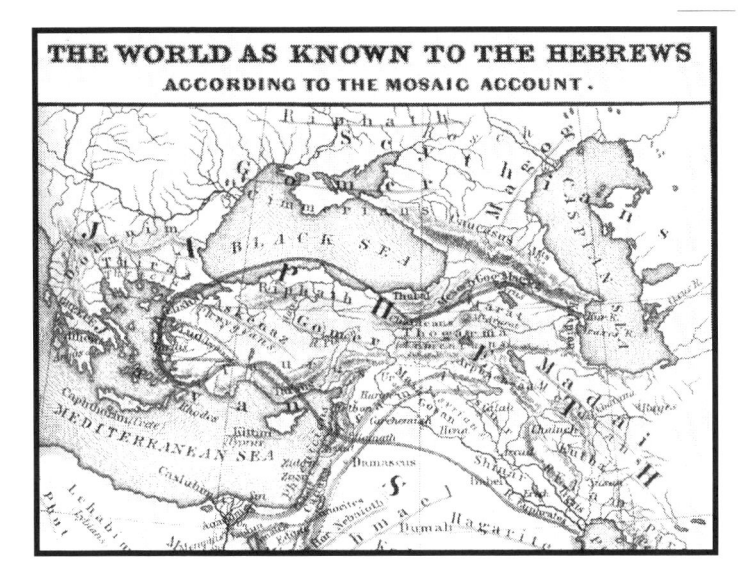

THE WORLD AS KNOWN TO THE HEBREWS
ACCORDING TO THE MOSAIC ACCOUNT.

> "Yahweh says: I am against you, O Gog, **chief prince** of Meshech and Tubal. ... Persia, Cush and Put will be with them, all with shields and helmets, also Gomer with all its troops, and Beth Togarmah from the far north with all its troops--the many nations with you' (Ezekiel 38:3-6).

Therefore, Turkey will be one of the ten who join with the other nine nations to form the Fourth Beast Kingdom which will later become the kingdom of the Antichrist.

So far we have identified five of the ten nations that will comprise the Fourth Beast Kingdom of the Antichrist.

1. Iraq
2. Egypt
3. Libya
4. Sudan, Northern
5. Turkey

Since there are many nations in the Middle East, Africa and Asia area which were part of Daniel's prophesies, let's look at a couple of common factors regarding the ten nations.

First, we should recognize that all ten are related to the Statue prophecy of Daniel chapter two. Daniel two gives us the historical perspective from **the head - ancient Babylon**, to **the ten toes – the final kingdom**.

Note: There are only four kingdoms mentioned in the statue prophecy and the first three are historical; Babylon, Media-Persia and Greece. This leaves only the fourth and final kingdom of the Antichrist which Daniel also described in chapters 7, 8, 9 and 11.

Note: Rome is not mentioned.

When we look at the geographical area historically encompassed by the enormous, dazzling statue of Daniel, we see more than ten nations.

Ten Nation Kingdom of the Antichrist

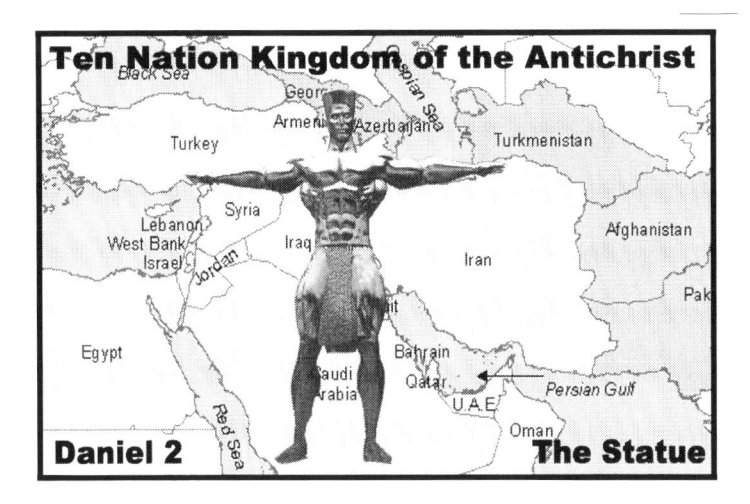

Daniel 2 — The Statue

There will, however, be only ten nations that join together to form the future kingdom of the Antichrist. Therefore, we must search the Scripture to see, what other factors will bind these ten nations together?

Second, besides geography what else do the prophets tells us about the ten that will enable us to find the other five?

All 10 Hate Babylon the Great

The prophet John was told about the identity of Mystery Babylon the Great and the Beast Kingdom on which she rides in Revelation 17. Here is how that is written.

> "I will explain to you the mystery of the woman [Babylon the Great] and of the beast [Antichrist] **she rides**, which has the **seven heads and ten horns.**" (Revelation 17:7)

As we read the Revelation 17 prophecy we should keep in mind that to "**sit on**" or "**ride" signifies a position of dominance**. Mystery Babylon is initially dominant over the Middle Eastern Kingdom. Therefore, the U.S.A. will keep her position of dominance until the Antichrist and his ten nation kingdom comes against the U.S.A. as we read below:

> "**The beast [Antichrist] and the ten horns you saw will hate** the prostitute (U.S.A.). **They will** bring her to ruin and leave her naked; they will eat her flesh and **burn her with fire.**" (Revelation 17:16)

The Antichrist and all ten kings will hate Babylon the Great and bring her to ruin by burning her with fire. So, who are the other five nations who will hate the U.S.A.? Today, the U.S.A. is becoming less and less popular in the Middle East. However, after the violence and destruction caused by the leader of the Babylonians as described in Habakkuk 2, many more nations will come to hate the U.S.A.

If I were to make an educated guess, I would add the following five nations to our list; Syria, Lebanon, Iran, Afghanistan and Pakistan.

If I'm correct the list of the ten will look like this:

1. Iraq
2. Egypt
3. Libya
4. Sudan
5. Turkey
6. Syria
7. Lebanon
8. Iran
9. Afghanistan
10. Pakistan

Now, let's take a look at the Antichrist himself.

II: Beast from the Middle East

What happens if more than one king arises to power from Iraq, how will we know the real Antichrist?

Will the real Antichrist stand up?

Once again, let's see what Scripture has to say. What other characteristics can we find regarding the Antichrist?

Ancestors of the Antichrist

Daniel tells us who the ancestors of the Antichrist were. They were the ancient Syrians who were part of General Titus' Roman Army in 70 A.D. They were the people who destroyed the city of Jerusalem and the Jewish Temple. Let's examine how Daniel explained who the people of the Antichrist would be.

> "The people **of the ruler who will come** will destroy the city and the sanctuary." (Daniel 9:26)

We know that "the ruler who will come" is the Antichrist, because the next verse in Daniel details his actions during the last seven years, before the End. Here is what it says about him:

"**He** [Antichrist] **will** confirm a covenant with many for one 'seven.' In the middle of the 'seven' **he will** put an end to sacrifice and offering. And on a wing of the temple **he will** set up an abomination that causes desolation, until the end that is decreed is poured out on **him**." (Daniel 9:27)

From these verses we can positively identify the Antichrist as "**the ruler who will come**" the "**he**" of Daniel 9:27.

From history we can identify "The people" who "will destroy the city and the sanctuary" of Daniel 9:26. They were the people of the Roman Army in 70 A.D. under the leadership of the Roman General Titus.

This is where many Bible teachers have made a "**Big Mistake**." They assume that the people in the Roman Army were Roman soldiers. But that is not what history recorded.

Fortunately, this part of Israel's history was very well documented. The Jewish historian, Josephus recorded the details of this time while he was in the employment of the Romans.

Josephus described how General Titus had given orders **not** to destroy the Jewish sanctuary, desiring that it remain as a trophy of his victory[8]. Never-the-less, when the final battle was being fought, fire got into the temple and burned the gold covered woodwork. In the heat of the fire the gold melted down into the cracks of the stonework.

Following the battle, the soldiers took down every stone to get at the gold which had melted into the stonework of the temple. This event is another amazing record of how precise God's prophecies are fulfilled. Here is what Christ prophesied about this, 38 years earlier.

> "Some of his disciples were remarking about how the temple was adorned with beautiful stones and with gifts dedicated to God. But Jesus said, "As for what you see here, the time will come when **not one stone will be left on another; every one of them will be thrown down**." (Luke 21:5-6)

Josephus also recorded who the soldiers were in Titus' army, the people responsible for the destruction of the city and sanctuary. He wrote that they were Syrians. Syria at that time was part of the Roman Empire and it encompassed present day Syria and Lebanon. Josephus also recorded that following Titus' campaign in Israel, the Syrian soldiers returned home with their loot (gold). At that time the price of gold in Syria dropped in half, due to the amount gold brought home by the Syrian soldiers[9].

From Josephus' historical account we can see that the people who destroyed the city and the sanctuary where ancient Syrians.

---

[8] Josephus: The Complete Works – Wars of the Jews 6.4.3

[9] Josephus: The Complete Works – Wars of the Jews 6.6.1

Therefore, "the ruler who will come," the Antichrist will be of ancient Syrian descent. The territory of Ancient Syria is today Lebanon and Syria. Therefore, the Antichrist's ancestors will be from either Lebanon or Syria.

What else can we know about the Antichrist?

What does Antichrist look like?

In Isaiah 10:12 we were told something about the Assyrian King's appearance. He has a haughty or proud look in his eyes. This is not the only place in prophecy that gives us an indication of the Antichrist's appearance. Here are two others examples from Daniel's prophecies:

> "I also wanted to know about … the horn [Antichrist] that **looked more imposing [stout] than the others and that had eyes** and a mouth **that spoke boastfully**." (Daniel 7:20)

> "In the latter part of their reign, when rebels have become completely wicked, a **stern-faced king**," (Daniel 8:23)

This is the Antichrist's appearance:

- He has a haughty or a proud look in his eyes.
- He looks more imposing than the other 9 kings.
- He has eyes that speak boastfully.
- He is a stern-faced king.

What else do we need to know?

Antichrist is like no other

In addition to what we have already learned, what else do the prophets say about the Beast King we call Antichrist?

Here are a few descriptions with scriptural references.

The Antichrist will:

- Try to change the set times and laws – Daniel 7:25
- Be a master of intrigue – Daniel 8:23
- Cause astounding devastation - Daniel 8:24
- Succeed in whatever he does – Daniel 8:24
- Cause deceit to prosper - Daniel 8:25
- Corrupt with flattery – Daniel 11:32
- Have no regard for the gods of his fathers – Daniel 11:37
- Greatly honor those who acknowledge him – Daniel 11:39
- Purpose to destroy – Isaiah 10:7
- Put an end to many nations – Isaiah 10:7

The Antichrist will not be a Christ like figure. Even though he will confirm a peace treaty, he will not be a peace maker. He will rule the whole world but he will not be the head of a mythical "One World Government" or a "New World Order." The Antichrist will be a military ruler and a destroyer of nations.

These prophecies help us understand about the Antichrist and his Middle-eastern kingdom with its **7 heads and 10 horns**. Armed with this information we will have little difficulty identifying this fourth beast kingdom and the Antichrist when they appear on the world scene.

We are over 12 years into the Time of the End. Therefore, today, the Antichrist is alive and well and living in Iraq.

For hundreds of years people have tried unsuccessfully to identify who the Antichrist will be. But, now that we are so close to the fulfillment of these prophecies about the Antichrist, perhaps we should take another look to see if there is anyone who currently meets the criteria and characteristics which have been prophesied.

First let's list the characteristics of the Antichrist.

Characteristics of the Antichrist:

- **Ancestry**: Ancient Syria. Present day Lebanon and Syria.

- **National ruler**: Ancient Assyria which is present day Iraq.

- **Personal Character**: A military leader who will honor a god of fortresses.

- **Physical Characteristics**: Stern-faced, haughty look, stout, more imposing than his peers.

There is one Middle-eastern Iraqi leader who meets some of the qualifications of the Antichrist. He is also, potentially, in a position to become the future leader of Iraq. That person is **Sayyid Muqtadā al-Sadr**. Let's compare him to the characteristics of the Antichrist and determine if he is the man.

Muqtada al-Sadr:

- **Ancestry**: Muqtada al-Sadr is of **Lebanese** ancestry.

- **National ruler**: Muqtada al-Sadr was born in Baghdad, Iraq. He is currently living in Iran where he became an **Ayatollah**. He is one of the most influential religious and political figures in Iraq. "Senior British officers were of the opinion that the radical cleric Muqtada al-Sadr, the leader of the Shia Mahdi Army, would enter the political process"[10] which he has.

- **Personal Character**: Muqtada al-Sadr is the founder and leader of the 60,000 man Mahdi Army in Iraq.

- **Physical Characteristics**: Muqtada al-Sadr is stern-faced, has a haughty look, and is stout and more imposing than other Middle-eastern leaders.

---

[10] http://www.independent.co.uk/news/uk/politics/british-troops-to-start-iraq-pullout-in-march-1059445.html

If Muqtada al-Sadr becomes the future leader of Iraq, he will also become the Antichrist. Newsweek magazine called him the most dangerous man in Iraq. If Muqtada al-Sadr fulfills the prophecies of the Antichrist, he will become the most dangerous man in the world.

What We Know About the Antichrist

- The Fourth Kingdom comes **before** the Antichrist.
- His ancestors will be from Lebanon or Syria.
- He will be from present day Iraq.
- He will cause the devastation of the U.S.A.

III: Beasts of Revelation 13

Now that we have a good biblical foundation regarding the Antichrist and his Middle Eastern Kingdom, let's examine Revelation 13 about the beast and his ally.

> "And the dragon stood on the shore of the sea. And I saw a **<u>beast</u>** coming out of the sea. **He had ten horns and seven heads**, with ten crowns on his horns, and on each head a blasphemous name. The beast I saw **resembled a leopard**, but had feet **like** those of **a bear** and a mouth like that of **a lion**. The dragon gave the beast his power and his throne and great authority." (Revelation 13:1-2)

Because, the beast (Antichrist) "had **ten horns and seven heads**" this vision is after the **Fourth Seal War** when Antichrist subdues three of the 10 heads; Egypt, Libya and Sudan.

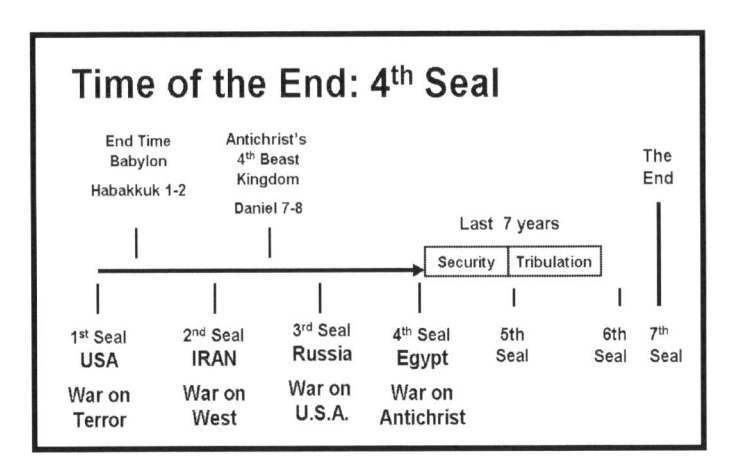

Time of the End: 4th Seal

End Time Babylon Habakkuk 1-2	Antichrist's 4th Beast Kingdom Daniel 7-8			Last 7 years Security | Tribulation		The End
1st Seal **USA** War on Terror	2nd Seal **IRAN** War on West	3rd Seal **Russia** War on U.S.A.	4th Seal **Egypt** War on Antichrist	5th Seal	6th Seal	7th Seal

There is another clue in this passage to where the Antichrist comes from. John wrote that the beast resembled a **leopard, bear and lion**. These, like the **ten horns and seven heads,** are also descriptions which we find mentioned in Daniel's prophecy regarding the kingdom of the Antichrist. Let's have a look.

> "The first (**Babylon) was like a lion**, and it had the wings of an eagle. ... And there before me was a second beast (**Media-Persia), which looked like a bear**. ... "After that, I looked, and there before me was another beast (**Greece), one that looked like a leopard.**" (Daniel 7:4-6)

Yahweh also used these three descriptions; "like a lion, leopard and bear" when He told Israel how He would come against them at the Time of the End, recorded in Hosea 13:4-10.

Again, we can know the area of the ten horn Kingdom from which the Beast known as Antichrist will arise.

What else does John tell us about the first beast?

> "One of the heads of the beast seemed to have **had a fatal wound**, but the **fatal wound had been healed**. The whole world was astonished and followed the beast. Men worshiped the dragon (Satan) because he had given authority to the beast, and they also worshiped the beast and asked, "Who is like the beast? **Who can make war against him**?" (Revelation 13:3-4)

It appears that the Antichrist will be killed and then raised from the dead. This is not done every day and it is easy to see why the whole world will be astonished.

This is one of those examples where it will be good for Yahweh's people to know their Bible prophecy. Other wise one might be deceived by this amazing miracle. Remember, Christ said, I've told you everything ahead of time.

The other thing is, "**Who can make war against him**?" As I said earlier, the beast is not Christ like, he will be a warrior king. What else is there?

> "The beast was given a mouth to utter proud words and blasphemies and to exercise his authority for **forty-two months (3.5 years)**. **He opened his mouth to blaspheme God**, and to slander his name and his dwelling place and those who live in heaven. He was given power to make **war against the saints and to conquer them**. And he was given authority over every tribe, people, language and nation. All inhabitants of the earth will worship the beast--all whose names have not been written in the book of life." (Revelation 13:5-8)

Here we are reminded that the Great Tribulation lasts 3.5 years (forty-two months**),** as we were told in Daniel's prophecy below:

> "He will speak against the Most High and oppress his saints and try to change the set times and the laws. The saints will be handed over to him for **a time, times and half a time (3.5 years).**" (Daniel 7:25)

Next, John introduces us to another beast. But, before he does he leaves this warning about the Great Tribulation.

> "If anyone is to go into captivity, into captivity he will go. If anyone is to be killed with the sword, with the sword he will be killed. **This calls for patient endurance and faithfulness on the part of the saints.**" (Revelation 13:10)

Second Beast: False Messiah

As John writes about this second beast he gives us some clues to his identity. First, John says that he comes "**out of the land**" which could be a reference to Israel the "promised land." The second clue says that he is "**like a lamb**."

> "Then I saw **another beast**, coming **out of the** earth **(land)**. He had two horns **like a lamb**, but he spoke like a dragon. He exercised **all the authority of the first beast** on his behalf, and made the earth (land) and its inhabitants worship the first beast, whose fatal wound had been healed. And he performed great and miraculous signs, even causing fire to come down from heaven to earth in full view of men." (Revelation 13:11-13)

As we examine the prophecies about Revelation's second beast there are some things we should keep in mind.

First, as the Messiah Himself indicated, there will be a False Messiah.

> "I have come in my Father's name, and you do not accept me; but if someone else comes in his own name, you will accept him." (John 5:43)

> "False Christs and false prophets will appear and perform great signs and miracles to deceive even the elect--if that were possible. See, I have told you ahead of time." (Matthew 24:24-25)

Second, the Antichrist will not be the False Messiah because he will not be Jewish and he will not be from Israel.

Third, as Christ said about Israel, "you will accept him" therefore, the False Messiah will be Israel's king during the Great Tribulation.

What else does John write about the False Messiah?

> "Because of the signs he was given power to do on behalf of the first beast (Antichrist), he deceived the inhabitants of the earth (land). He ordered them to set up an image in honor of the beast who was wounded by the sword and yet lived. He was given power to give breath to the image of the first beast, so that it could speak and cause all who refused to worship the image to be killed." (Revelation 13:14-15)

So far John has indicated that this second beast will perform miraculous signs on behalf of the Antichrist and he will cause people to worship the Antichrist. Next John tells us about the mark of the Antichrist also known as the "Mark of the Beast."

> "He (False Messiah) also forced everyone, small and great, rich and poor, free and slave, to receive a mark on his right hand or on his forehead, so that no one could buy or sell unless he had the mark." Revelation 13:16-17)

With the information we have received so far, we can be certain that the second beast of Revelation 13 is the man who John called the False Prophet in Revelation 19. Let's see what John wrote to confirm that he is, the False Prophet.

> "But the beast (Antichrist) was captured, and with him **the false prophet (*pseudoprophetes*)** who had **performed the miraculous signs** on his behalf. With these signs he had deluded those who had received the mark of the beast and worshiped his image." (Revelation 19:20)

The Greek word *pseudoprophetes* means false prophet or religious impostor. Therefore, *pseudoprophetes* could also indicate a False Messiah as well as a false prophet. What other information does John reveal about this False Prophet that will help us know who he will be when he appears in Israel?

John tells us that the False Prophet works closely with the Antichrist and that they both go to their destruction when the real Messiah returns.

> "Then I saw three evil spirits that looked like frogs; they came out of the mouth of the dragon, out of the mouth of the beast (Antichrist) and out of the mouth of **the false prophet**. They are spirits of demons performing miraculous signs, and they go out to the kings of the whole world, to gather them for the battle on the great day of God Almighty." (Revelation 16:13-14)

> "But the beast (Antichrist) was captured, and with him **the false prophet** who had performed the miraculous signs on his behalf. ... **The two of them were thrown alive into the fiery lake of burning sulfur.**" (Revelation 19:20)

I hope you have noticed as we have been going through Revelation's prophecies that we have drawn heavily on the Old Testament prophets to help us understand what John was saying. Once again we are going to look to the prophets to help us understand who this "second beast" and "false prophet" will be.

The prophets also saw that the "False Messiah," the "King of Israel" would be destroyed when the real Messiah showed up. Here is what Hosea wrote about that day.

> "Sow for yourselves righteousness, reap the fruit of unfailing love, and break up your unplowed ground; for it is time to seek Yahweh, until he comes and showers righteousness on you. … Thus will it happen to you, O Bethel, because your wickedness is great. When that day dawns, **the king of Israel will be completely destroyed.**" (Hosea 10:12, 15)

Once again the prophets help us understand. The Antichrist will be the Beast from the Middle East and the False Messiah will be the "King of Israel."

One last thing before we move on. After the Antichrist proclaims himself to be God, the False Prophet begins to force everyone to take the mark of the beast.

> "He also forced everyone, small and great, rich and poor, free and slave, to receive a mark on his right hand or on his forehead, so that no one could buy or sell unless he had **the mark, which is the name of the beast or the number of his name**. This calls for wisdom. If anyone has insight, let him calculate the number of the beast, for it is man's number. His number is 666." (Revelation 13:16-17)

I do not know what the "mark of the beast" will be. However, after all the wars which will occur before the Great Tribulation, it would not surprise me if the "mark of the beast" turns out to be a simple tattoo of the name or number of the Antichrist.

There is something I noticed years ago about the number 666.

We already know that the Antichrist proclaims that he is God at the "abomination that causes desolation" in the Temple of Yahweh in Jerusalem. When he does this it will no doubt cause a great deal of commotion and violence in the temple and in Jerusalem. The prophet Isaiah seems to capture this situation in his **666** prophecy.

> "Hear that uproar from the city, hear that noise from the temple! It is the sound of Yahweh repaying his enemies all they deserve." (Isaiah **66:6**)

Also, all the chapter and verse numbers in the Bible are man's numbers. Man put the numbers in the Bible, not Yahweh. Never the less, Yahweh knew what numbers would go with what verses.

Richard H. Perry

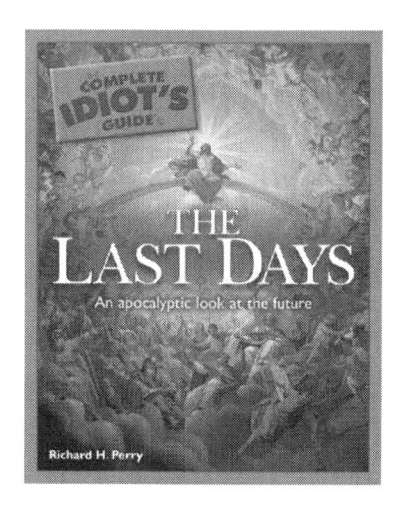

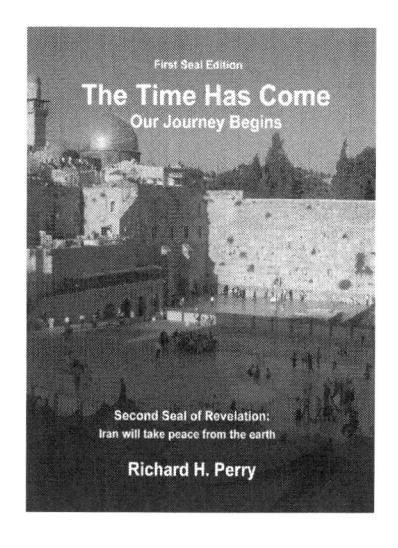

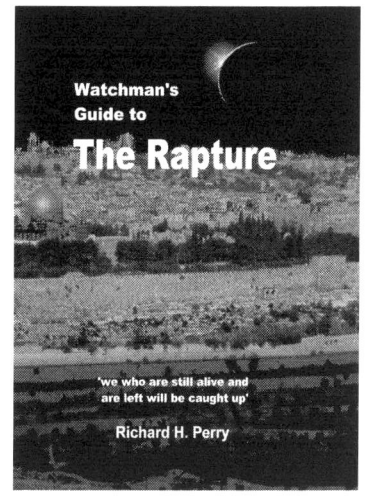

179

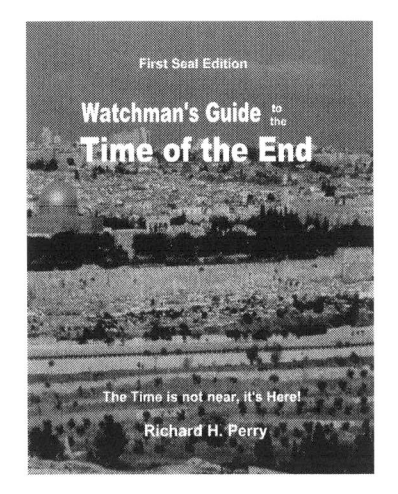

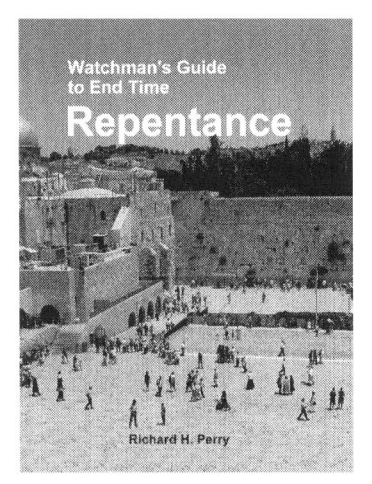

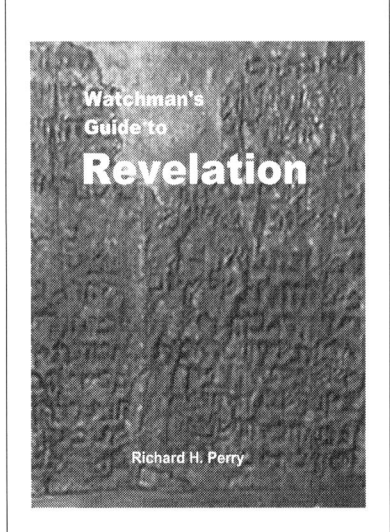

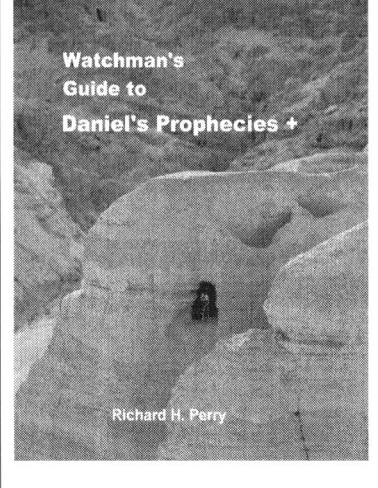

Made in the USA
Charleston, SC
05 July 2013